IDAHO

OFF THE BEATEN PATH®

Praise for previous editions of *Idaho Off the Beaten Path*®

"Rushing around Idaho is inherently pointless . . . you can
miss the spirit and the majesty in an unplanned moment,
the unexpected person, the odd place, off the beaten path."
—*USA Today*

"[This book] makes traveling across the state exciting,
whether you're taking the kids up to college at Moscow
or heading over to Idaho Falls to visit Grandma."
—*Idaho Statesman*

OFF THE BEATEN PATH® SERIES

NINTH EDITION

IDAHO

OFF THE BEATEN PATH®

DISCOVER YOUR FUN

JULIE FANSELOW

Globe
Pequot

Guilford, Connecticut

For Natalie: born to travel, rooted in Idaho

Globe
Pequot

An imprint of Rowman & Littlefield

Off the Beaten Path is a registered trademark of Rowman & Littlefield

Distributed by NATIONAL BOOK NETWORK
800-462-6420

Copyright © 2017 Julie Fanselow
Maps: Equator Graphics © Rowman & Littlefield

British Library Cataloguing in Publication Information is available.
ISSN 1535-4431
ISBN 978-1-4930-2785-9 (paperback)
ISBN 978-1-4930-2786-6 (ebook)

∞™ The paper used in this publication meets the minimum requirements of American National Standard for Information Sciences—Permanence of Paper for Printed Library Materials, ANSI/NISO Z39.48-1992.

All the information in this guidebook is subject to change. We recommend that you call ahead to obtain current information before traveling.

Contents

About the Author

Julie Fanselow lived in Idaho for more than twenty years and still returns regularly to see what's new. Her other books include *Traveling the Lewis and Clark Trail* and *Traveling the Oregon Trail* (Globe Pequot), and she contributes to many national and regional magazines.

Acknowledgments

Many Idahoans too numerous to name recommended special spots throughout the Gem State for this book. My thanks to all. I'd also like to acknowledge the staff of the Idaho Department of Commerce and everyone at the local chambers of commerce and visitors bureaus who keep me up-to-date on what's happening around Idaho. Thanks, too, to the people at Globe Pequot/Rowman & Littlefield and the editors at *Journey, Sunset, Hemispheres, Where to Retire,* and *Via* magazines, for whom I've written about Idaho.

Special thanks to Bruce Whiting and Natalie Fanselow Whiting. Natalie was a baby when I first researched this book. She had visited nearly every Idaho county by her first birthday, and she is finishing college in Boise as this latest edition is published. This book remains dedicated to her, as well as to the memory of my father, Byron Fanselow, who gave me a love for travel and accompanied me to many of the places in this book.

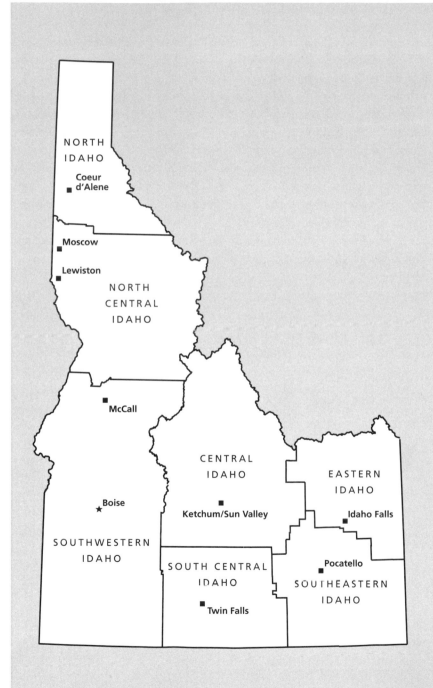

NORTH
IDAHO

Coeur
d'Alene

Moscow

Lewiston

NORTH
CENTRAL
IDAHO

McCall

CENTRAL
IDAHO

EASTERN
IDAHO

Ketchum/Sun Valley

Idaho Falls

Boise

SOUTHWESTERN
IDAHO

SOUTH CENTRAL
IDAHO

Pocatello

SOUTHEASTERN
IDAHO

Twin Falls

Introduction

When I first moved to Idaho, I had about two weeks before I was scheduled to start my job at the newspaper in Twin Falls. What better way to spend the time, I figured, than on a quick orientation trip around my new home state? Two weeks would be plenty of time to take a drive through Idaho's mountainous midsection, followed by a beeline for the Canadian border, a detour through Montana to Salmon, and a swing through Eastern Idaho.

Or so I thought. A week or so later, I'd meandered across maybe a quarter of my intended route. As someone who had grown up on the fringes of Pennsylvania suburbia and come of age in rural Ohio, I knew more than a little bit about back roads and small towns. But I knew next to nothing about a landscape that would force me, by virtue of geography and scenery, to really slow down and savor the journey, not to mention a piece of huckleberry pie here and a buffalo burger there. Years later, I still haven't seen nor experienced all Idaho has to offer—especially not now, when international cuisines are joining mountain fare on the state's menus and an increasingly urban Idaho has as many cultural delights as recreational destinations. I expect it will take a lifetime, and that's fine.

In a sense, all of Idaho could be considered off the beaten path. It's true that here—like elsewhere—interstates now cross the state from east to west. But Highway 12, the only route across North Central Idaho, didn't link Lewiston to Missoula, Montana, until 1961. The White Bird Grade on the state's only major north–south road, US 95, wasn't completed until 1975. When the highway is closed by bad weather or rock slides, travelers must make a five-hour detour through Oregon and Washington. And until the early 1990s, it was nonstop cross-country from Boston to Seattle on Interstate 90, except for one stoplight in the town of Wallace, Idaho.

Idaho was the last of the continental United States to be settled by whites pushing westward (although Native Americans were here 10,000 to 15,000 years ago). When pioneers pressed west on the Oregon and California Trails, most kept right on going through what would become Idaho. When British fur traders staked their claims in the Northwest, they did so hundreds of miles west near the mouth of the great Columbia River. Idaho's first permanent town, Franklin, wasn't settled until 1860, and many communities didn't exist at all until early in the twentieth century.

Despite its slow start, Idaho is one of the fastest-growing states in the nation, especially in the Boise metropolitan area, home to about four out of every ten Idahoans, and near Coeur d'Alene. But no matter where you are in Idaho, you don't have to travel far to escape: Owyhee County, south of Boise, and the Central Idaho Rockies, northeast of the capital city, remain so sparsely settled they could qualify as frontier. All across Idaho, residents and visitors have plenty of opportunities to get happily lost for a day, a weekend, or longer, on a seldom-traveled forest road, in an abandoned mountaintop fire tower, in a country antiques store, or in a tucked-away cafe. I also believe you can venture off the beaten track in cities and towns, so this book also includes lesser-known and offbeat places in Idaho's larger communities.

A few notes on how to use this book: There are seven chapters, each covering one of the tourism regions designated by the Idaho Travel Council. Each chapter leads off with a general overview of the region. With roads few and far between in many areas of Idaho, it is impossible to avoid retracing a route once in a while, but I've tried to keep backtracking to a minimum. Although each chapter leads off with a general map of the region and its attractions, you will want to use a more detailed map in planning your travels. You can get a free highway map by calling (800) VISIT-ID (847-4843). Maps are also available at visitor centers, via visitidaho.org, or by writing the Idaho Travel Council at 700 West State St., Boise 83720. For more detailed maps, the *Idaho Atlas & Gazetteer* published by DeLorme Mapping (delorme.com) or the *Idaho Road & Recreation Atlas* (benchmarkmaps.com) are both good choices, as are the maps published by the various units of the US Forest Service in Idaho.

The State of Idaho's travel website at visitidaho.org has lots of resources to help you explore the state. You can read themed travel articles, order printed copies of the latest state maps and brochures, and sign up for an e-mail newsletter for people who like to travel in the Gem State. The state has a strong social media presence, too, so check out its pages on Facebook, Instagram, and so on. I've also set up a Facebook page for this book. Visit facebook.com/idaho guidebook to see my latest discoveries and share your own Idaho travel tips.

If, like many Idahoans and visitors, you're here mainly for Idaho's riotously abundant recreational and adventure sports opportunities, there are several good resources online. Idaho has more federally designated wilderness lands—nearly four million acres—than any other state in the Lower 48, with an additional nine million acres of roadless public land. Much of Idaho is, therefore, accessible only by boat, on horseback, on foot, or by chartered plane flown into a backcountry airstrip. For more information about exploring Idaho's wilderness areas, contact the ***Idaho Outfitters and Guides Association*** at (800) 49-IDAHO or ioga.org. If you are specifically interested in the Middle Fork of the Salmon River, Idaho's world-renowned raft trip, check out idahosmiddlefork .com for a list of outfitters and trip-planning information. For a Meetup site listing hikes for all interests and abilities, see idahohikingclub.com.

Adventuring 101

Many children—and adults, too—spend most of their lives indoors these days, and the idea of being outside can be a bit intimidating. *Idaho State Parks' First Time Adventure Program* offers special experiences for people who've always wanted to try bird-watching, Dutch oven cooking, fishing, camping, paddling, and more. Instruction and gear are provided, so these are good try-before-you-buy opportunities if you're intrigued but not quite ready to commit to an outdoor hobby. See parksandrecreation .idaho.gov for details on participating parks and activities.

The state park system also offers an annual passport—a motor home or passenger vehicle sticker, available for $10 when you register or renew your vehicle—that gets Idaho residents into all state parks for a year and discounted camping, too. (Out-of-staters can buy an annual vehicle entry pass for $40. It also covers all state parks and gives holders a discount on camping fees.) Regular state park motor vehicle entrance fees are $5, and campsites cost about $15 to $45 a night depending on location and services offered.

It's still possible to travel 50 miles or more in Idaho without passing a gas station, and cell phone service remains weak in many areas. Just because a town is listed on a map or road sign, that's no guarantee you'll find a filling station or other services there. So before you set out off the beaten path, make sure your vehicle is in good shape and the fuel tank is full. Carry a good full-size spare tire and jack, a gasoline can, and a basic emergency kit, including flashers. A shovel and ax also can come in handy on unpaved back roads, the former in case you encounter a snowdrift, the latter in the event a tree has fallen in your path. (Both these things happen not infrequently on Forest Service roads in Idaho's high country, even in the dead of summer.) Most of the places mentioned in this book are accessible using any two-wheel-drive vehicle in good condition, but a few are unsuitable for large RVs or vehicles towing trailers. When in doubt, inquire locally before setting off on an unfamiliar back road.

I've tried to list prices for most attractions, but bear in mind these are subject to change. Use the prices as a guideline, and call ahead for updates or more information. The listings at the end of each chapter are a small representative sampling of what you'll find in each region, and a listing doesn't necessarily imply an endorsement of the business. Room rate categories reflect double occupancy in high season. Restaurant cost categories refer to the price of a single entree without beverage, dessert, taxes, or tip. Because prices change all the time, these are guidelines. Updated information for most places is usually available online.

Restaurants

$12 or less	Inexpensive
$13 to $20	Moderate
$21 and over	Expensive

Places to Stay

Under $75	Inexpensive
$75 to $150	Moderate
$151 to $250 per night	Expensive
$251 and up a night	Very Expensive

Although you won't find any Airbnb listings in this book, I am a big fan of the popular site that lets people book stays in private homes world-wide. Sometimes you want a traditional hotel or motel room, but Airbnb accommodations come in a much wider price range and in some really cool locations. Hosts and travelers alike are reviewed to ensure safety, and most hosts are happy to engage with their guests, or not, depending on travelers' preferences. There are also many Idaho listings on Vacasa.com, VRBO.com, and HomeAway.com, among other home-sharing sites. (Note, too, that many bed-and-breakfast inns and even a few motels are now listing their businesses on one or more home-rental sites as a way to stay competitive in the rapidly shifting lodging landscape.) If you are new to home-sharing sites, pay attention to whether you're renting a room or a whole house. And always check cancellation policies; house rules on things like smoking and pets; and especially cleaning fees, which vary considerably and can be the same whether you stay a night or a week.

Camping is big in outdoorsy Idaho, and many state parks and private campgrounds also have accommodations for people who aren't towing a trailer or toting a tent. Small cabins, cottages, yurts, and luxury "glamping" tents in these parks generally run from $50 to $100, making them good values. For ideas, see rvidaho.org and idahostateparks.reserveamerica.com.

Also remember that Idaho, unique among states, is divided north–south into two time zones. The northern part of the state—everything north of Riggins, if you're driving US 95—is on Pacific time, while the south runs on Mountain time.

It is my hope that *Idaho Off the Beaten Path* will inspire you to hit the open road and discover this great state. Whether you seek an unusual family vacation destination, a romantic weekend rendezvous, or a fun one-day get-away; whether you desire mountain peaks, high desert stillness, or crystalline lakes, Idaho awaits your exploration. If, in your own travels, you come across changes in the information listed here or a great place that might be mentioned in a future edition of this book, drop me a line at juliewrites@yahoo.com, note it at facebook.com/idahoguidebook, or write me in care of Globe Pequot, 246 Goose Lane, Guilford, CT 06437. Thanks—and happy travels!

Idaho Facts

POPULATION (2015 ESTIMATE)

- 1,654,930

STATEWIDE TOURISM INFORMATION

- (800) VISIT-ID or visitidaho.org

MAJOR NEWSPAPERS AND WEBSITES

- *The Idaho Statesman* (Boise): idahostatesman.com

- *Boise Weekly* (alternative news and views): boiseweekly.com

- *Idaho Press-Tribune* (Nampa): idahopress.com

- *The Times-News* (Twin Falls): magicvalley.com

- *The Idaho State Journal* (Pocatello): idahostatejournal.com

- *The Post Register* (Idaho Falls): postregister.com

- *The Coeur d'Alene Press*: cdapress.com

- *Lewiston Morning Tribune*: lmtribune.com

- *The Spokesman-Review* (North Idaho): spokesman.com

HELPFUL STATEWIDE PHONE NUMBERS AND WEBSITES

- State of Idaho home page: accessidaho.org

- Idaho weather: wrh.noaa.gov

- Traveler information and road conditions report: Dial 511 or (888) 432-7623 or visit 511.idaho.gov

- Idaho Department of Parks and Recreation: (208) 334-4199 or parksandrec reation.idaho.gov

- Idaho Department of Fish and Game: (208) 334-3700 or idfg.idaho.gov

- United States Forest Service: (208) 373-4100 or fs.fed.us

- Idaho RV Campgrounds Association: (208) 345-6009, (800) RV-IDAHO, or rvidaho.org

- State and federal agencies also have a robust presence on social media sites, especially Facebook, and many also have mobile apps.

MORE FAST FACTS

- Idaho's population didn't reach 1 million until 1990. By 2014 it had risen to 1.6 million people, making it one of the nation's fastest-growing states.

- Idaho has more white water than any other state, with about 3,100 miles of river rapids.

- Idaho is the only state with an official seal designed by a woman, Emma Edwards Green.

- Idaho elected the nation's first observant Jewish governor, Moses Alexander, in 1914.

- Yes, Idaho is the nation's leading potato producer. But you knew that.

Transportation

AIR

Getting to and from Idaho usually involves a layover or two and travel on smaller aircraft, though there are some direct flights. Idaho's major airport is in Boise, which has scheduled service from Alaska, Allegiant, American, Delta, Horizon, SkyWest, Southwest, and United Airlines. Several companies including McCall Air and Gem Air offer regular service to backcountry gateway towns from Boise, too. See more information at iflyboise.com. Other airports with scheduled service include Hailey (Sun Valley), Idaho Falls, Lewiston, Twin Falls, and Pocatello. Many people traveling to North Idaho choose to fly into Spokane, Washington (just 33 miles from Coeur d'Alene). And the airport in Salt Lake City (161 miles from Pocatello) is reasonably convenient to destinations in the Southeastern, Eastern, and South Central regions of Idaho.

BUS

You can take an intercity bus to nearly thirty cities and towns in Idaho, including Boise, Cascade, Coeur d'Alene, Idaho Falls, Lewiston, McCall, Moscow,

Pocatello, Riggins, and Twin Falls. Greyhound service on the US 95 corridor and into Eastern Washington is by Northwestern Trailways, a partner company. For more information call (800) 231-2222 or visit greyhound.com.

SHUTTLE

Salt Lake Express (based in Rexburg, Idaho) provides scheduled service to destinations across Idaho's southern tier, as well as Jackson, Wyoming, and West Yellowstone, Montana. Call (208) 656-8824 or see saltlakeexpress.com for routes and prices.

TRAIN

Amtrak's Empire Builder route passes through Sandpoint in North Idaho twice a day. The eastbound train from Seattle arrives at 2:30 a.m., and the one coming west from Chicago pulls in around midnight. See amtrak.com for details.

Climate

Because Idaho is so big, its climate cannot be easily summed up in a paragraph. But generally Idaho is drier than the Pacific Northwest and milder than the rest of the Rocky Mountain region. In Boise, daytime highs range from about 90°F in July to the mid-30s in January, with nighttime lows in the 50s in summertime and the 20s December through February. In the panhandle region, summer daytime temperatures are typically in the 80s, dipping to about 50°F at night. In the winter expect North Idaho daytime highs at just about the freezing mark and lows about 20°F. Humidity is low around most of the state.

Precipitation varies widely, from only 9 inches of rain and 17 inches of snow falling annually at Twin Falls in South Central Idaho to 30 inches of rain and 75 inches of snow at Sandpoint. The best time to visit depends on your interests, but generally spring and fall are especially pleasant in the southern regions, while mid-July through mid-September are the best times to visit North Idaho and the Central Idaho mountains. The high country often has snow until after the Fourth of July.

Famous Idahoans

Famous Idahoans past and present include Edgar Rice Burroughs (author of *Tarzan*), Philo Farnsworth (who helped invent television), baseball great Harmon Killebrew, former Mormon church president Ezra Taft Benson (who also served as US Secretary of Agriculture), writers Ezra Pound and Anthony Doerr, musicians Josh Ritter and Curtis Stigers, Olympic medalists Kristin Armstrong and Picabo Street, Joseph Albertson (who started the grocery chain bearing his name), cable news personality Lou Dobbs, Mount Rushmore sculptor Gutzon Borglum, and actress Lana Turner. Other past and present celebrities who have made homes in the state include Jamie Lee Curtis, Patty Duke, Ernest Hemingway, Patrick McManus, Tom Hanks, Steve Miller, Demi Moore, Ashton Kutcher, George Kennedy, Scott Glenn, Arnold Schwarzenegger, and Bruce Willis.

Recommended Reading

TRAVEL AND OUTDOOR ADVENTURE

Boise Trail Guide: 90 Hiking and Running Routes Close to Home by Steve Stuebner (Boise Front Adventures, 2015). Stuebner has also written regional guides to mountain biking near McCall and paddling the Payette River. See more of his adventure travel tips at stevestuebner.com.

BigLife is a glossy quarterly magazine based in Sun Valley that covers "the big lives we live in the mountains" and mountain towns throughout the West. It's available in stores and online at biglifemag.com.

For 91 Days in Idaho by Jürgen Horn and Michael Powell. Three months' worth of blog posts about travel in Idaho circa 2012, collected into an e-book available via idaho.for91days.com.

Hiking Idaho by Ralph and Jackie J. Maughan and Luke Kratz (3rd edition; FalconGuides, 2014). A classic statewide guide that describes more than 100 trails.

Idaho for the Curious by Cort Conley (Backeddy Books, 1982; rereleased in 2003). This fascinating, weighty book concentrates on history along the state's highways.

No Bar Too Far: Idaho by Rich and Debbie Higgins (Not Too Far Publishing, 2013). A guide to the watering holes of Idaho, including jokes, trivia, drink recipes, and more.

Southwest Idaho Camping Guide by Roger Phillips and Pete Zimowsky (Idaho Statesman, 2009). The *Statesman*'s outdoor writers describe 45 campgrounds within a few hours' drive of the Boise area.

Traveling the Lewis and Clark Trail and *Traveling the Oregon Trail* by Julie Fanselow (Globe Pequot, 2007 and 2001, respectively). These books are comprehensive modern travel guides to the famous trails, both of which run through Idaho.

HISTORY

Big Trouble: A Murder in a Small Western Town Sets Off a Struggle for the Soul of America by J. Anthony Lukas (Simon & Schuster, 1997). A long but worthwhile examination of early Idaho labor strife.

Building Idaho: An Architectural History by Jennifer Eastman Attebery (University of Idaho Press, 1991).

Camera Eye on Idaho by Arthur A. Hart (Caxton Press, 1990). A fascinating survey of pioneer photography in the state from 1863 through 1913.

In Mountain Shadows by Carlos Arnaldo Schwantes (University of Nebraska Press, 1991). An incisive look at how Idaho was shaped by divisions in geography, politics, religion, and more.

Roadside History of Idaho by Betty Derig (Mountain Press Publishing, 1996).

NATURAL HISTORY

Birds of Idaho Field Guide by Stan Tekiela (Adventure Publications, 2003).

Roadside Geology of Idaho by David Alt and Donald W. Hyndman (Mountain Press, 1989).

Rocks, Rails and Trails by Paul Karl Link and E. Chilton Phoenix (Idaho Museum of Natural History, 1996). A photo-packed look at the geology, geography, and history of Eastern and Southern Idaho. It's also available online at imnh.isu.edu/digitalatlas.

LITERATURE AND MISCELLANEOUS

Angle of Repose by Wallace Stegner (Doubleday, 1971). Based on a book of letters by Idaho writer Mary Hallock Foote, this Pulitzer Prize–winning novel traces a family's journeys across the frontier West. Foote's letters, collected as *A Victorian Gentlewoman in the Far West* (Huntington Library Press, 1992), make a good companion volume.

Daredevils by Shawn Vestal (Penguin, 2016). Evel Knievel's 1974 visit to the Snake River Canyon is among the plot lines in this well-reviewed novel by a writer who grew up nearby.

Housekeeping by Marilynne Robinson (Picador, 2004). Originally published in 1980, Robinson's tale of sisters growing up in Fingerbone (modeled on Sandpoint) won a PEN/Hemingway Award for best first novel.

Idaho 24/7 edited by Rick Smolan and David Elliot Cohen (Dorling Kindersley, 2004). Many of Idaho's top photographers contributed to this day-in-the-life document of life statewide.

Idaho Loners: Hermits, Solitaries, and Individualists by Cort Conley (Backeddy Books, 1994). Idaho is a state of individualists, and veteran writer Conley interviewed some of the most singular for these profiles.

Idaho's Poetry: A Centennial Anthology edited by Ronald E. McFarland and William Studebaker (University of Idaho Press, 1989).

Small Town Ho: The Hilarious Story of Moving from the Big City to North Idaho by Duke Diercks (Slog Press, 2016). Despite the cringe-worthy title, this is a genuinely funny book about a family's move from Texas to Idaho. Also set in Sandpoint, though that's where the similarity to *Housekeeping* ends.

Where the Morning Light's Still Blue: Personal Essays about Idaho edited by William Studebaker and Richard Ardinger (University of Idaho Press, 1994).

Written on Water: Essays on Idaho Rivers edited by Mary Clearman Blew (University of Idaho Press, 2001).

FOR CHILDREN

Idaho (Hello USA series) by Kathy Pelta (First Avenue Editions, 2002).

P Is for Potato: An Idaho Alphabet by Stan and Joy Steiner and Jocelyn Slack (Sleeping Bear Press, 2005).

North Idaho

For decades the lakes of North Idaho were a private playground for the people of the Northwest. If you grew up in eastern Washington, Idaho, or Montana, chances are your family vacationed on the shores of Lake Coeur d'Alene at least once. If you didn't, your neighbors probably did. But outside this corner of the country, few people had North Idaho on their radar screens.

Today, however, North Idaho has been discovered. Coeur d'Alene and Sandpoint are hot spots. Even scruffy old Wallace and Kellogg, long the victims of declining mining fortunes, are enjoying a tourism-centered renaissance. Consequently, you may need to work a bit harder to get off the beaten path in this region. But it can be done.

Interstate 90 runs through Coeur d'Alene and the Silver Valley surrounding Wallace, and it's the only high-speed road in the region. Elsewhere, even on US 2 and 95, two-lane stretches, stunning scenery, and occasionally heavy traffic are apt to slow you down. If you'd really like to leave the crowds behind, try the road up the east side of Priest Lake, the Coeur d'Alene Scenic Byway (Highways 97 and especially 3), or Highway 200 east of Sandpoint (the Pend Oreille Scenic Byway). These routes are part of the *International Selkirk Loop,*

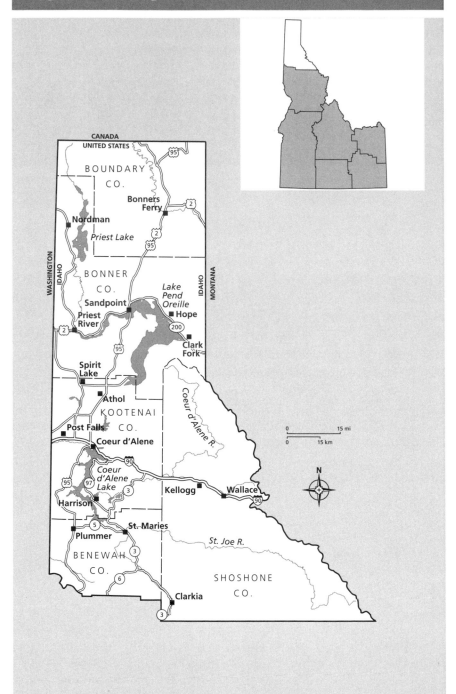

CANADA
UNITED STATES

BOUNDARY CO.

Bonners Ferry

Nordman

Priest Lake

BONNER CO.

Lake Pend Oreille

Sandpoint

Priest River

Hope

Clark Fork

Spirit Lake

Athol

KOOTENAI CO.

Post Falls

Coeur d'Alene

Coeur d'Alene R.

Coeur d'Alene Lake

Harrison

Kellogg

Wallace

St. Maries

Plummer

BENEWAH CO.

Clarkia

St. Joe R.

SHOSHONE CO.

WASHINGTON

IDAHO

IDAHO

MONTANA

0   15 mi
0   15 km

N

a 280-mile scenic byway that connects Idaho and Washington with British Columbia. *Sunset* magazine once called the loop the Northwest's most scenic drive, and it's hard to argue. The route is remote, yet there are enough towns and services along the way to fill a long weekend or even a week's road trip. For more info on the route, call (208) 267-0822 or visit selkirkloop.org.

For more North Idaho travel information, call (208) 664-3194 or look at visitnorthidaho.com.

Lakes and Forests

Everywhere you look in North Idaho, you see either dense forests, expansive lakes, or both. This part of the state is most noted for its three large lakes—Coeur d'Alene, Pend Oreille, and Priest Lake (which actually is two lakes)—and the recreation-oriented resort towns on their shores. But rivers also run through this country, their Native American names music to the ears, their wild rapids and placid pools pure tonic for the soul. Two of these rivers—the Kootenai and the Moyie—meet at Bonners Ferry, the seat of Boundary County. East of town under a bridge spanning US 2, the Moyie flows through one of Idaho's most impressive canyons. The 1,223-foot-long steel truss **Moyie River Bridge,** built in 1964, is the second highest in the state, just 12 feet shy of the Perrine Bridge over the Snake River Canyon at Twin Falls. Stop at the rest area just east of the bridge for a good view of the span, or take the road to Upper and Lower Moyie Falls, two cascades that drop 100 feet and 40 feet, respectively.

Also along the Moyie River is **Snyder Guard Station,** a cabin first used as a forest ranger headquarters in 1908. Today the cabin is one of several available for rent from the Idaho Panhandle National Forests. The guard station, available May through Dec, is listed on the National Register of Historic Places. Sleeping arrangements can accommodate about a dozen people indoors and more outside camping in tents or RVs; plus you'll get electric heat, running

AUTHOR'S FAVORITES IN NORTH IDAHO

Under the Sun
Bonners Ferry

Sierra Silver Mine Tour
Wallace

Lake Pend Oreille
Sandpoint

Trail of the Coeur d'Alenes
Mullan to Plummer

Coeur d'Alene's Old Mission State Park
Cataldo

water for hot showers, and a kitchen—all for $50 a night for one to six people or $70 a night for seven to fifteen people. A horse corral outside makes this a fine equestrian retreat, too.

To reach Snyder Guard Station, head north on US 95 from Bonners Ferry; turn right about 27 miles north at Good Grief, Idaho; and go 4 miles south on County Road 34, the Moyie River Road. See recreation.gov for availability and reservations for this cabin and many others throughout Idaho.

West of Bonners Ferry, the 2,774-acre **Kootenai National Wildlife Refuge** serves as an oasis to migrating waterfowl and a bird-watcher's paradise. In spring look for mallards, pintail, American widgeon, and tundra swans. Canada geese visit in August and September, while the mallards fly through later in the fall. All summer you may see cinnamon and blue-winged teal, common goldeneyes, and wood ducks. Wildlife spotted at the preserve include moose, muskrats, deer, beaver, and more.

The refuge is open to visitors during daylight hours year-round. In addition to excellent wildlife watching, you'll find some nice, short hiking trails. To find the refuge, drive 5 miles west of Bonners Ferry on Riverside Road. Stop at the refuge entrance for a self-guiding map to the refuge's foot trails and a 4.5-mile driving tour. For more information call (208) 267-3888 or visit kootenai.fws.gov.

Idaho is a remote state, and its people are self-sufficient. Because Bonners Ferry is 535 miles from Boise, the state capital, and a good two-hour drive from the nearest metro area, people know how to make do for themselves. So it's no surprise that there are some real finds in Bonners Ferry's tiny downtown. **Under the Sun** at 7178 Main St. is a wonderful twenty-first-century general store (open from 8 a.m. to 5 p.m.; closed Sun) with housewares, gifts, clothing, and more. A small cafe in the back serves lunch, with mostly organic soup, salad, and sandwich fare. **Groove Studio** at 7169 Main St. features a good selection of works by local artists. **Bonners Books** at 7195 Main St. has been supplying Idaho's far north with eclectic new and used reading material for decades, and it's also a good source for local topographic maps.

North Idaho is hops country, and the **Kootenai River Brewing Company** uses the local crop plus swift-running Selkirk Mountain water to brew fresh, small-batch beer. Stop by its taproom and restaurant at 6424 Riverside St. For an overnight stay in Bonners Ferry, choices include a few standard motels plus the **Northside School Bed and Breakfast,** where host Ruth Perry was once a student. Built in 1914, the hilltop schoolhouse has nine themed rooms (all with full bathrooms), a heated pool, and a hot tub. Rooms start at about $80 in the off-season and $140 May through Oct. Call (877) 222-1826 or see northsideschoolbedandbreakfast.com.

Echoes of Ruby Ridge

Randy Weaver and his family moved to remote North Idaho in 1983 to live off the land, practice a radical brand of Christian fundamentalism, and turn up at the occasional gathering of the state's fringe neo-Nazi movement. Because most Idahoans have a live-and-let-live philosophy, the Weavers didn't attract much attention—until 1990, when Randy was caught selling illegal arms to an undercover Bureau of Alcohol, Tobacco, and Firearms agent. Released after a court appearance, he decided to hole up on his property and make the law come to him.

After a year and a half of surveillance, federal marshals moved in. It's never been proven who shot first, but by the time the gunfire ended, three people were dead: decorated US Marshal William Degan; Weaver's fourteen-year-old son, Samuel; and Weaver's wife, Vicki, who was holding her baby when she fell. Following an eleven-day standoff, Weaver surrendered. He subsequently went to trial on murder and conspiracy charges, beating all but a failure-to-appear rap with the aid of flam-boyant defense attorney Gerry Spence. Weaver left Idaho and eventually relocated to Montana with his daughters, after receiving an out-of-court settlement from the federal government to conclude a wrongful death lawsuit he filed.

As a young reporter for the *Spokesman-Review* newspaper, Jess Walter covered the standoff—which took place near Naples, south of Bonners Ferry—and eventu-ally wrote a book about it. *Every Knee Shall Bow*, later titled *Ruby Ridge: The Truth & Tragedy of the Randy Weaver Family*, sweeps the reader along like a novel—and indeed, Walter is now better known as a novelist whose books include *Beautiful Ruins* and *The Financial Lives of the Poets*.

Six miles south of Bonners Ferry, the **Blue Lake RV Resort** is beloved for its swimming hole, a summertime wine bar, and Wi-Fi. The resort has spots for your camper or tent, as well as two "glamping" options. The Lilly Pad is a lake-side platform tent with electricity, a woodstove, and a queen log bed. The Dog-wood Cottage has a deck overlooking the lake. Each costs about $50 a night or $300 for a week. Call (208) 946-3361 or have a look at bluelakervresort.com.

Western Pleasure Guest Ranch is among Idaho's oldest guest ranches, in business and in the same family since 1940. Located well off the highway between Bonners Ferry and Sandpoint, it has great views of the nearby Cabinet and Selkirk mountain ranges. In summertime, Western Pleasure offers an all-inclusive seven-night package for $1,950 per person ($1,650 for children ages 6 through 12). Fall through spring, there are bed-and-breakfast stays from $125 a night for two people and cabin rentals starting at $180 a night for up to four people. If you're just passing through or staying elsewhere in the area, you can arrange for a few hours on horseback or a wintertime sleigh ride. For more information, call (888) 863-9066 or see westernpleasureranch.com.

Although much smaller than Coeur d'Alene, Sandpoint rivals its neighbor as the most interesting town in North Idaho. Sandpoint's abundant natural attractions include Lake Pend Oreille, Idaho's largest, and **Schweitzer Mountain Resort.** Schweitzer is one of the West's biggest ski areas, with nearly 3,000 skiable acres; that and its fairly remote location help make it one of the least crowded. From the top, skiers are treated to unbeatable views of Lake Pend Oreille. At the bottom, guests can relax in a slopeside room or condo or party in Sandpoint. Schweitzer has a full range of offerings in the warmer months, too. Summertime visitors can ride a chairlift, picnic atop the mountain, try geocaching, go mountain biking, or play golf. For more information on Schweitzer, call (208) 263-9555 or visit schweitzer.com.

US 95 used to run right through downtown Sandpoint, backing up traffic for blocks. In 2012 a bypass was completed, so things are a bit sleepier now, but Sandpoint remains one of Idaho's most interesting towns to explore on foot. As part of the bypass project, Sandpoint also gained several miles of paved trails along Lake Pend Oreille and Sand Creek, so park your vehicle and stroll around. There are interesting shops galore in the compact downtown, plus abundant public art. (Don't miss the open-air **Galaxy Gallery** in the alley between First and Second Avenues.)

Sandpoint's pride and joy is the **Panida Theater,** originally opened in 1927 and dedicated to "the people of the Panhandle of Idaho," thus the name. (It rhymes with Canada.) For years the Panida was considered one of the premier movie palaces of the Northwest, but like many theaters, it fell on hard times in the late 1970s and early 1980s. The community rallied to buy and restore the Panida, and it's now home to a full calendar of films and performing arts. The Panida is at 300 North First Ave. Call (208) 263-9191 or visit panida .org for upcoming events. Nearby, **The Hive** at 207 North First Ave. is a top venue for touring bands. Look for the drumstick door handles, and see who's going to be onstage at livefromthehive.com.

Another local preservation success story, the **Cedar Street Bridge Public Marketplace** began life as an actual bridge in the 1930s. After nearly falling apart by the late 1970s, the bridge was reimagined in the 1980s as Idaho's answer to the Ponte Vecchio marketplace in Florence, Italy. In the 1990s it became the flagship location for Sandpoint-based clothing retailer Coldwater Creek, which took over the entire bridge in its heyday. Today the bridge once again hosts small shops, several restaurants, and a drop-in family art studio. See cedarstreetbridge.com for a current business directory.

A few blocks from the downtown core, **Foster's Crossing Mall** at 504 Oak St. is a rambling old building stuffed with antiques and collectibles. Head southwest from there via the Little Fox Trail bike/hike path to reach Sand-

TOP ANNUAL EVENTS IN NORTH IDAHO

Sandpoint Winter Carnival
(Feb)

Depot Days
Wallace (early May)

Independence Day Celebration
Kellogg (July 4)

Festival at Sandpoint
(Aug)

Art on the Green
Coeur d'Alene (first weekend in Aug)

Coeur d'Alene Tribal Pilgrimage to Cataldo
(Aug 15)

North Idaho State Fair
Coeur d'Alene (late Aug)

point's emerging **Granary Arts District**. (You'll know it by the big grain storage building along Church Street.) **Evans Brothers Coffee Roasters** at 524 Church St. took third place in the 2015 America's Best Coffeehouse competition in Portland, Oregon. There are usually food trucks parked nearby, too.

The **Festival at Sandpoint**, a concert series held midsummer on Lake Pend Oreille, features an inspired menu of music ranging from roots rock to the Spokane Symphony Orchestra. See festivalatsandpoint.com for upcoming shows and tickets.

Ponderay, a small community just north of Sandpoint, serves as the gateway to Schweitzer Mountain, and it has a few indie business gems amid its mix of chain stores, restaurants, and motels. Spokane-based Ruby Hospitality has its first Idaho outpost on the site of a former Motel 6 at **Hotel Ruby Ponderay,** a moderately priced boutique motel at 477255 US 95 North, with an indoor pool and bicycles to borrow. Rates start at about $75. Call (208) 263-5383 or see hotelrubyponderay.com. **Laughing Dog Brewery,** one of North Idaho's oldest craft brewers, has its taproom and pup-friendly patio at 1109 Fontaine Dr.

Highway 200 heads east from Sandpoint toward Montana. If you're looking for Hope, look no further: It's about a twenty-minute drive east of Sandpoint via Highway 200. Near here, in 1809, Canadian explorer David Thompson established Kullyspell House, the earliest fur trade post in the American Pacific Northwest. Nothing remains of the post, but a monument to Thompson's efforts sits along the highway. The **Old Ice House Pizzeria & Bakery** at 140 West Main St. in Hope serves up thin-crust New York–style pies, plus sweets including baklava, muffins, and cookies, all with a lake view. The phone number is (208) 264-5555.

If your idea of camping comfort includes an airy cabin with wood-planked floors and a quilt-topped queen-size bed plus a heated private outdoor shower (but no Wi-Fi or TV or even electricity), you'll appreciate **Huckleberry Tent and Breakfast** near Clark Fork, also east of Sandpoint on Highway 200. Its three canvas-walled tents rent for $119 to $139 a night and include a hearty breakfast. You'll also enjoy meeting Christine and Tim Dick, who homesteaded this land in the 1990s and are eager to share what they've learned as modern-day pioneers who grow their own food and get power from the sun. Call (208) 266-0155 or learn more at huckleberrytentandbreakfast.com.

West of Sandpoint, Lake Pend Oreille narrows into a river along US 2. **Dover Bay Resort** is a pretty spot with beach bungalows and larger vacation homes for rent and an upscale casual restaurant, Dish, that has waterfront dining for lunch, dinner, and summer Sunday brunch. The community's trails and parks are open to all, and it's a nice spot for a picnic.

A half-hour drive west from Sandpoint, the town of Priest River is showing signs of life in its small downtown. Browse for fine art and folk art at the **Artisan Gallery** at 53 Wisconsin St. and check out the improvements and shops at the **Beardmore Block** at 119 Main St. Originally built in 1922 by Charles Beardmore, the historic building—including its Rex Theatre—has been restored by his great-grandson, architect Brian Runberg.

Head north from Priest River to **Priest Lake,** North Idaho's least-used big lake. Named for the Jesuit priests who came to the region to spread their gospel among the Native Americans, Priest Lake is bordered to the east by the Selkirk Mountain Range, whose more than 7,000-foot peaks stand majestic against the lake's altitude of some 2,400 feet above sea level. Priest Lake is actually two lakes—the main body of water and Upper Priest Lake, which is connected to the much larger lower lake by a 2-mile-long water thoroughfare. Area marinas rent boats and other watercraft that can be used to ply the lakes and thoroughfare as well as explore island campsites dotting the water. The eastern shore is almost entirely undeveloped save for **Priest Lake State Park** and a few marinas. Nevertheless, this was where Nell Shipman—an early silent film star—had a studio during the 1920s, way up at Lionhead on the lake's northeastern tip.

At the south end of Priest Lake, the **Old Northern Inn** welcomes vacationers to a gracious, antiques-filled bed-and-breakfast. Amenities include a small private marina, a swimming and sunning beach, and a deck overlooking the lake. The inn is open Memorial Day through mid-Oct, with four rooms and two suites, all with private baths. Rates range from $115 to $175 double occupancy, including a home-cooked breakfast for two. Children over age 12 are welcome. For more information or reservations, call (208) 443-2426 or see oldnortherninn.com.

The west side of Priest Lake has more commercial development than the east side, but still nothing compared to the shores of Coeur d'Alene and Pend Oreille. **Hill's Resort** has been welcoming guests to Luby Bay since 1946 and has won wide acclaim for catering to families. Aside from water-based activities, Hill's is accessible to good hiking, mountain biking, volleyball, golf, tennis, hunting, cross-country skiing, and about 400 miles of groomed snowmobile trails. And then there's the food. Baby back ribs, pistachio-crusted halibut, and huckleberry pie are among the specialties, and the view of Priest Lake is a welcome side dish. Hill's has a wide range of hotel rooms, condos, and cabins priced by the night or the week. Call (208) 443-2551 or see hillsresort.com for reservations or more information.

Huckleberries are plentiful in Northern Idaho, and some of the best berry patches are located along Priest Lake. Because huckleberries need sunlight to ripen, the best picking is often along abandoned logging roads and areas opened to sunshine by forest fires. Look for shrubs about 1 to 5 feet tall, with tiny pink or white urn-shaped flowers that blossom in June or July. The berries themselves are purplish black to wine red in color, and they generally ripen in July or August, although some berries on slopes facing north may linger as late as October.

Humans like huckleberries a lot, but so do black bears and grizzly bears. The Selkirk Mountains are one of a handful of places where the legendary grizzlies still range in the United States, so caution must always be used. (Wear bells, keep a clean camp, and retreat from the area should a bear turn up.) Search online for the Idaho Panhandle National Forests' Priest Lake Ranger District to see a map of berry-picking areas.

State Highway 57 ends at Nordman, but a 14-mile trip up Forest Road 302 (the West Side Road) leads to the **Roosevelt Grove of Ancient Cedars**, where you can see a virgin forest of trees ranging up to 2,000 years old. Short hiking trails from the grove lead to views of Upper and Lower Granite Falls.

Although the big lakes are best known in North Idaho, a few smaller bodies of water are noteworthy. **Round Lake State Park** has shaded campsites near its fifty-eight-acre lake and summertime rentals for canoes, paddleboats, and stand-up paddleboards. Get more info at parksandrecreation.idaho.gov/parks/round-lake. Nearby, **Hoodoo Creek Cafe** is a friendly little place with breakfast, burgers, wraps, and more, plus camping provisions. Follow Dufort Road 7 miles west from the state park, then turn left on Vay Road and drive another mile until you see the cafe.

In the town of Spirit Lake, the **White Horse Saloon, Hotel & Cafe** at 6248 West Maine St. claims to be the oldest continually operating saloon in Idaho, open since 1907. It has five rooms with shared bathrooms priced at $50 and three rooms with their own bathrooms for $70. See thewhitehorsesaloon.com or call (208) 623-2353 for more info. About a mile from the small downtown, the *Spirit Lake Rec Center* has kayaks, canoes, paddleboards, and bikes for rent starting at $10 an hour and $25 for a half-day. It's open weekends starting Memorial Day weekend and seven days a week by mid-June.

At Hauser Lake, just a few miles north of bustling Post Falls, *Embers by the Lake* has taken over the former Chef in the Forest location, replacing its predecessor's upscale fare with gourmet pizza. It's open for dinner Wed through Sat at 12008 North Woodland Beach Dr.

The Coeur d'Alenes

With a population of about 145,000 people and its proximity to the Spokane metro area, Kootenai County has a suburban, bedroom community feel. Strip malls and subdivisions predominate, and the area is gaining favor with retirees, too, with its mix of abundant recreation and strong medical services.

Post Falls stretches along I-90 from the Washington state line to Coeur d'Alene. In the downtown area, amiable chef Raci Erdem presides over two popular and lively restaurants. "You love garlic. We love you," promises the streetside mural outside *The White House Grill* at 712 North Spokane St. Greek, Turkish, and Italian fare is on the menu here, all heavy on the garlic (and feta, too). *The Oval Office,* Erdem's other eatery, has a wider bistro-style menu and a martini bar. It's at 620 North Spokane St. Both are open daily.

On a hot day many Post Falls residents can be found at *Q'Emilin Park,* with its grassy lawn and beach. (Q'Emilin, pronounced "ka-MEE-lin," is a Native American term that means "throat of the river.") Few, however, know that a magnificent canyon nearby awaits exploration. The gorge is also home to an outcropping of rocks popular with local rock climbers. To find the canyon, just stroll back beyond the boat dock and parking area.

One of Idaho's most storied state parks is near the town of Athol at the south end of big Lake Pend Oreille. In 1941 the US Navy built the second-largest naval training center in the world on this site at the foot of the Coeur d'Alene Mountains. Over fifteen months during World War II, 293,381 sailors received basic training at Farragut Naval Training Station. Following the war the site served for a time as a college before being transformed into *Farragut State Park* in 1965. Since then the park—one of Idaho's largest—also has hosted several national Boy Scout and Girl Scout gatherings.

The park visitor center displays exhibits detailing the Navy presence at Farragut, which hasn't disappeared entirely: The military still uses 1,200-foot-deep Lake Pend Oreille as a submarine testing site. But recreation reigns at Farragut these days, with good opportunities for camping, hiking, cross-country skiing, boating, and wildlife viewing. Mountain goats patrol the steep peaks along Pend Oreille's south shore, and deer, moose, elk, and bear are also in residence. Farragut State Park is open year-round, with a $5-per-vehicle state park admission charge. For information call (208) 683-2425 or visit parksand recreation.idaho.gov/parks/farragut.

It might be a stretch to call the Northwest's largest amusement park a truly off-the-beaten-path attraction, especially when it sits along US 95 about 20 miles north of Coeur d'Alene. But **Silverwood Theme Park** is out of the way for the thousands of urbanites who drive many hours here for summer fun. Silverwood offers plenty to make the trek worthwhile, including several top-notch roller coasters and the Boulder Beach water park, plus an old-school railroad ride and Vegas-style magic shows in the "Theater of Illusion." Silverwood admission, which includes both the amusement park and Boulder Beach, runs about $48 for visitors age eight and up and about $25 for children ages 3 to 7 and senior citizens, with evening and two-day discounts available. See silverwoodthemepark.com or call (208) 683-3400 to plan a visit.

If a day at Silverwood isn't in the budget, or you want something more low-key, **Honeysuckle Beach** is a local favorite. Aside from offering a popular boat access point to Hayden Lake, this park—just 2 miles from US 95—has a

Comfy Camping

Not everyone likes to sleep on the ground, and not everyone has camping equipment. If you fit either category, you can still enjoy Idaho's state parks by reserving one of the camping cabins, which are available at parks throughout the state.

The year-round cabins, which measure 12 feet square, can sleep up to five people for $55 a night. They're furnished with log-style beds, a table and chairs, lamps, power outlets, heat (and even air-conditioning in some locations), lockable windows and doors, and a porch complete with swing. A fire ring and picnic table are situated outside each cabin, and restrooms, water, and showers are located nearby. Campers bring their own sleeping bags, cookware, and eating utensils. The wheelchair-accessible cabins are perfect for people with disabilities, too.

Cabins are available at these state parks: Bruneau Dunes, Dworshak, Farragut, Hells Gate, Henrys Lake, Heyburn, Lake Walcott, Massacre Rocks, Priest Lake, and Three Island Crossing. Older cabins and yurts are available in several parks, too. For complete information or reservations, see idahostateparks.reserveamerica.com. Idaho also has several dozen cabins and lookouts available for rent on US Forest Service land. To find them, search at recreation.gov. Some are extremely rustic; others have complete kitchens and even indoor plumbing.

small sandy beach with a lifeguard. A pathway leading from the satellite parking lot has several good spots for fishing from the banks. It's a wonderful place for walking your dog, too.

As a major tourist destination and the commercial center for North Idaho, Coeur d'Alene is packed with restaurants, art galleries, and shopping opportunities. Sherman Avenue between Fourth and Sixth Streets is the best place to start your explorations. Among the many restaurants, **The Cellar** at 317 East Sherman Ave. has wine flights, plates to share, and a name-your-price chef's tasting menu featuring fresh seasonal fare at $30, $40, or $50 per person. **Crafted Tap House and Kitchen** at 523 East Sherman Ave. is a hot spot for beer (with fifty taps) and gastropub grub, plus turtle races every Friday night at 10 p.m. Its huge patio on the corner of Sherman and Sixth is perfectly placed to overlook the summer revelry that is Live After 5 (Wednesday evenings until 8:30) and 1st Friday Funk. The **Blackwell Boutique Hotel** at 820 East Sherman Ave. is a favorite wedding venue and perhaps the most convenient place to stay downtown, with nine plush rooms, lovely grounds, and a wraparound porch.

Coeur d'Alene has Idaho's highest concentration of bed-and-breakfast inns. Among them the **Roosevelt Inn** consistently gets high marks. This handsome former schoolhouse, listed on the National Register of Historic Places, has been a bed-and-breakfast since 1994. Guests here have access to a twenty-four-hour hot tub and spa, a CD library, snacks and beverages, and lots of books, plus

Eat a Burger

Coeur d'Alene has lots of swanky, high-end restaurants, but if you enjoy a good burger, this town has them in abundance. Here are a few of the best:

Hudson's Hamburgers at 207 East Sherman Ave. is classic Coeur d' Alene, a tiny spot with a simple menu and burgers that *Sunset* magazine listed among the tops in the West. It's been open since 1907. No shakes, no fries, but you can get a side of homemade hot sauce for that burger plus a slice of pie for dessert.

Moon Time, a neighborhood-style pub about a mile from the lakefront at 1602 Sherman Ave., has excellent traditional hamburgers plus a wonderful vegetarian option: the Anasazi Bean Burger, with a side of roasted corn pasta salad and a Moon Unit brownie for dessert. Moon Time also has live music and cheap pints of beer every Thurs night.

Finally, there's **Adventures in Deliciousness,** a bright yellow food truck parked beside a tire shop at 3033 North Government Way, open Tues through Sat. The name pretty much says it all, and locals swoon for the pure Angus beef burgers as well as the macaroni-and-cheese bacon balls.

it's only a short walk to downtown or Lake Coeur d'Alene. Room rates start at about $189 and include a gourmet breakfast. For more information call (800) 290-3358 or see therooseveltinn.com.

The Coeur d'Alene Resort often makes lists of the top resorts in the continental United States. The Coeur d'Alene isn't exactly off the beaten path—its copper-topped presence dominates the city's lakefront—but it does have one amenity no other resort in the world can claim: the ***Floating Green*** on the resort golf course. The brainchild of resort co-owner Duane Hagadone, the green is a par three on the fourteenth hole. It's also a moving target, floating between 100 and 175 yards from the blue (longest) tees. The movement is controlled by a computer, with the hole's length displayed each day at the tee. More than 30,000 golfers play the course each year, and during one memorable season, 22,000 golf balls, 50 golf clubs, and a couple of golfers landed in the lake. The golf balls are removed from the lake weekly by salvage divers, but there's no word on what happens to errant golf clubs or golfers!

The Coeur d'Alene Resort Golf Course is notable for other elements of its design, too. The links were constructed on the site of a former sawmill, and planners strove to incorporate as much of the natural environment into the course as possible. An osprey nest perches on a piling beside the thirteenth tee, and Fernan Creek and its trout spawning beds parallel the eleventh fairway. For these efforts the course was given a special award for environmental sensitivity from the Urban Land Institute. The Coeur d'Alene golf experience doesn't come cheap, though fees can be as low as $125 (or as high as $250) depending on your tee time. The greens fee includes eighteen holes, caddy service, a luxury GPS-equipped golf cart for each twosome, range balls, tees, and a personalized bag tag. Stay-and-play packages are available. For more information or reservations, see golfcda.com/tee-times or call (800) 935-6283.

Coeur d'Alene's City Park is a summertime magnet, with beachfront fun and boardwalks to stroll. If it's too bustling for your taste, head instead to ***Tubbs Hill,*** a 120-acre wooded city park on the peninsula just southeast of downtown. The main trail on Tubbs Hill begins on the west side at the south end of Third Street; from there, spur trails provide access for great hiking. Dogs are allowed on a leash. For more information on Tubbs Hill, call the city parks department at (208) 769-2252.

Another quiet spot is The Nature Conservancy's ***Cougar Bay Preserve,*** featuring eighty-eight acres of wetlands along the northwest shore of Lake Coeur d'Alene. Visitors will find more than 5 miles of hiking trails and a canoe-kayak launch. Many critters make homes here, including waterfowl, shorebirds, songbirds, moose, beaver, otter, and deer. The preserve entrance is about 2 miles south of Coeur d'Alene on US 95; look for the sign on the left (east) side of the road. The boat access area is about three-quarters of a mile north of the entrance. More information is available from The Nature Conservancy at (208) 676-8176.

The oldest standing building in Idaho is preserved handsomely at *Coeur d'Alene's Old Mission State Park,* accessible via exit 39 off I-90. The Sacred Heart Mission was primarily built between 1848 and 1853, the work of Coeur d'Alene Indians laboring under the supervision of Father Antonio Ravalli, a Jesuit missionary. The tribe called the mission "The House of the Great Spirit." The Coeur d'Alene Indians welcomed the Jesuits, for they believed the "Big Prayer" brought by the priests would give them an advantage over their enemies. There proved to be many parallels between the Native Americans and the Catholics: Each had a sense of the miraculous, the crucifix and rosaries were akin to the Indians' sacred charms, the chants of the Jesuit priests weren't unlike the natives' tribal songs, and the Catholics' incense, like the Indians' sage, was said to help carry prayers skyward.

Ravalli designed the mission in classical Roman Doric style. In addition to serving as architect, he helped adorn the inside with devotional paintings and European-style chandeliers fashioned from tin cans. Wooden ceiling panels were stained blue with huckleberry juice to resemble the sky. Incredibly, when the Coeur d'Alenes were sent to a reservation, the boundaries drawn did not include their beloved mission. A new mission was built at DeSmet, 60 miles away. But the Sacred Heart Mission (also called the Cataldo Mission) remains an important site for history buffs. Explore exhibits detailing the encounters between the black robes and the native peoples, or attend a special event such as the Coeur d'Alenes' annual pilgrimage to the site for the Feast of the Assumption. This event, held every August 15, includes a Mass, barbecue, and Native American dancing. Other annual happenings include a Historic Skills Fair with living history demonstrations the second Sunday each July and a Mountain Man Rendezvous the third weekend of August. Old Mission State Park is open year-round 9 a.m. to 5 p.m. Admission is $5 per vehicle. Phone (208) 682-3814 or see parksandrecreation.idaho.gov/parks/coeur-d-alenes-old-mission for more information.

Coeur d'Alene's Old Mission State Park is also the headquarters for the *Trail of the Coeur d'Alenes,* a 72-mile paved path among the longest of its kind in the United States. In an innovative solution to an environmental problem, the asphalt trail seals what was once the heavy metals-contaminated Union Pacific railroad bed between Mullan and Plummer. The mostly flat trail is open for cycling, skating, and pedestrian use. The state and the Coeur d'Alene Tribe both manage it.

The nicest stretch of trail is the 40 or so miles between Enaville and the old Chatcolet Bridge south of Harrison. Here, the trail runs far from I-90, winding along the Coeur d'Alene River and numerous lakes. Bike rentals and lodging are available in Kellogg and Harrison, among other towns, and picnic waysides dot the route. Be sure to carry drinking water and snacks. Many cycling enthusiasts combine the Trail of the Coeur d'Alenes and the Route of the Hiawatha near Wallace (see the next section) for a great bike-based vacation in North Idaho. For maps or more information, see friendsofcdatrails.org and parksandrecreation.idaho.gov/parks/trail-coeur-d-alenes. Local resident Estar Holmes is the author of *Trail of the Coeur d'Alenes Unofficial Guidebook,* a good resource for lots more information on biking or hiking the route. Find out more and see where to get a copy at southlakecda.com.

The small town of Harrison has become a hub of activity and tourism for the Trail of the Coeur d'Alenes. Vacationing cyclists and birders rule the roost at the **Osprey Inn** at 134 North Frederick Ave., which was built as a rooming house for lumberjacks in 1915. Its five guest rooms each have a private bathroom, and three of the rooms include lake views. Rates run from $125 to $165 in summer, less in the off-season, including breakfast. For information or reservations call (208) 689-9502 or see ospreybnb.com.

Nearby, the **Cycle Haus** at 101 Coeur d'Alene Ave. has an espresso stand plus bike rentals priced from $20 for two hours, a bit more for recumbent bikes and trikes or bicycles built for two. It's open 8 a.m. to 8 p.m. June through Aug, with rentals by reservation in spring and fall. Call (208) 689-3436 or visit thecyclehaus.com.

Silver and Garnets

For more than a century, Idaho's Silver Valley—also known as the Coeur d'Alene Mining District—was the undisputed world leader in silver, lead, and zinc production. By 1985, a hundred years after mining began, the region had produced one billion ounces of silver, and the total value of wealth coaxed from the mines had topped $5 billion. But as mining fortunes have fluctuated in recent decades, the Silver Valley—like many Western communities formerly dependent on natural resources—is looking to recreation and tourism to rebuild its economy. The region's location along I-90 has proven a blessing, with many attractions visible from the freeway, but a few places require a detour from the highway.

The **Snake Pit** is one such spot. Dining in this restaurant is kind of like eating at a flea market. The walls are covered with collectors' plates, NASA memorabilia, and black velvet paintings, and patrons sit at extra-rustic furniture amid bulbous tree burls. The decor isn't to everyone's taste, but the food keeps people coming back. The special here is Rocky Mountain Oysters. ("These ain't from the sea. We will have them as long as the bulls cooperate," the menu cautions.) Other options include steaks, seafood, and buffalo burgers. Look for prime rib specials starting at 4 p.m. on Fri and an all-you-can-eat seafood buffet from 4 to 8 p.m. Sat.

There are plenty of stories about how the Snake Pit (sometimes called the Enaville Resort or Josie's) got its name. One popular tale recalls when water snakes used to inhabit the area around the outdoor privies used before indoor plumbing came along. Patrons occasionally caught the snakes, put them in a container, and brought them inside. The business also served as a way station for railroaders, miners, and loggers. In addition to food, they sometimes sought female companionship, and the women available at the roadhouse were supposedly called "snakes." The Snake Pit is open daily for lunch and dinner, with breakfast, lunch, and dinner served Sat and Sun. It's located 1.5 miles from exit 43 off I-90, up the Coeur d'Alene River Road. For more information call (208) 682-3453.

Sitting atop the old, mostly dormant Bunker Hill Mine in Kellogg, *Silver Mountain* resort has made a name for itself with the world's longest single-stage, people-carrying gondola. Each car transports eight people on a nineteen-minute, 3-mile ride that covers 3,400 vertical feet. The gondola runs in the summer as well as in the winter. After reaching the top, many warm-weather riders like to either hike or bike down the mountain on trails that range from 2 to 22 miles long. Skiers have their choice of more than seventy runs covering 1,600 acres. Silver Mountain also includes a year-round indoor water park, *Silver Rapids,* mainly intended for guests of the resort's Morning Star Lodge. Silver Rapids' signature attraction, the FlowRider, unleashes 60,000 gallons of water per minute into a "wave box" that simulates the thrills of surfing, skateboarding, and snowboarding. Visitors looking for tamer pleasures will enjoy the 315-foot lazy river, and there are dedicated areas for little kids to splash around, too. For more information on Silver Mountain, call (866) 345-2675 or visit silvermt.com.

Kellogg is doing its best to augment Silver Mountain with other attractions. Its small downtown features some interesting locally owned shops such as *Bitterroot Mercantile,* which stocks everything from Idaho-made goods to birdhouses and many beautiful antiques. It's at 117 McKinley Ave. *Moose Creek Grill* at 12 Emerson Lane (near the corner of East Portland Avenue and South Division Street) is the fancy dinner spot in Kellogg, with fresh seafood, good steaks, and handmade pasta. It's open Wed through Sun for dinner, with outdoor seating in the summer. Check out the menu at moosecreekgrill.com and call (208) 783-2625 for reservations and for seasonal closings.

Leave the interstate at exit 54 east of Kellogg to see the **Sunshine Mine Memorial,** which recalls the worst United States hard-rock mining disaster since 1917. On May 2, 1972, a fire broke out in the mine and, although eighty-five made it out safely and two were later found alive, ninety-one people died in the blaze. The monument features a miner hoisting a jack leg and a poem penned by then–state senator Phil Batt (later Idaho's governor). Small memorials placed by the miners' families are scattered beneath the trees on each side.

Wallace, Kellogg's neighbor to the east, is also eager to mine tourism gold by showcasing its historic glory days. The entire town is listed on the National Register of Historic Places, and *Budget Travel* magazine named it one of the "10 Coolest Small Towns in America." The area is well worth a day or more of exploration.

Wallace was the epicenter of another major Northwestern disaster, the August 1910 fires that burned more than three million acres in just two days. A 2-mile hiking trail along Placer Creek showcases the heroics of Ed Pulaski, the forest ranger who led his crew of forty-five men into an abandoned mine where they were able to survive the blaze. (Timothy Egan tells this story and others in his best-selling book *The Big Burn: Teddy Roosevelt and the Fire That Saved America*.) Ask at the **Wallace Visitors Center** at 10 River St. for directions to the trail, and allow two to three hours for the hike.

The other must-stop in Wallace is the **Sierra Silver Mine Tour,** the only one of its kind in North America. Visitors ride a trolley-style bus to the mine portal, where hard hats are issued for the trip underground. Once in the mine the tour guides—themselves experienced miners—talk about and demonstrate the pneumatic-powered equipment and techniques used to mine silver ore. Interestingly this mine was once used as a working classroom for Wallace High School students who wanted to pursue a career underground.

Along with the mine visit, tour patrons are treated to a drive-around orientation of Wallace. The seventy-five-minute tours leave every thirty minutes from 420 Fifth St. in Wallace. Tours are given from 10 a.m. to 4 p.m. June through Aug and from 10 a.m. to 2 p.m. in May and Sept. Cost is $15 for adults, $13 for senior citizens age 60 and up, and $8.50 for children ages 4 to 16. Bring a jacket because mine temperatures average about 50°F. For more information or to get advance tickets online, see silverminetour.org.

Just down the street from the mine tour office, the **Wallace District Mining Museum** at 509 Bank St. is a good spot to learn more about the mining industry and other area history. A short film, *North Idaho's Silver Legacy*, is packed with interesting tales from Wallace's past. Exhibits include several mine models, a beautiful local history quilt, and the world's largest silver dollar (3 feet in diameter, with a weight of 150 pounds). It's also the final resting place of "Old Blinky," which until 1991 was the last stoplight on I-90 between Seattle and Boston.

The mining museum has a gift shop and ample parking and is open daily from 9 a.m. to 5 p.m. May through Sept and daily from noon to 5 p.m. Oct through Apr. The cost is $3 for adults, $1 for kids ages 6 to 15, or $7 for a family. For more information call (208) 556-1592 or see wallacemining museum.org.

Wallace is a good spot for antiques shopping, with several stores arrayed along Bank Street. The **Wallace Brewing Company** at 610 Bank St. sends its tasty beers to bars and restaurants around the Northwest, but you can get its craft brews even fresher in its Orehouse Tasting Room, open daily in the afternoon and early evening. Learn more at wallacebrewing.com. If you've always wanted to do yoga at a brewery, this may be the place: See the events calendar on the website for info on classes held here once a month or so.

Train fans will enjoy a stop at the **Northern Pacific Depot Railroad Museum** at 219 Sixth St. in Wallace. The last train ran out of the Wallace depot

Idaho on Film

Lights . . . camera . . . disaster! With its wide range of unspoiled scenery, Idaho has landed some major roles in Hollywood, although it sometimes seems the state's involvement in movies has calamitous connections of one sort or another.

For example, the town of Wallace served as the setting for *Dante's Peak*, the 1997 exploding volcano film starring Pierce Brosnan and Linda Hamilton. Despite lukewarm reviews, Wallace is proud of *Peak*, and you can still buy souvenirs of the film at some businesses around town. The same can't be said for *Heaven's Gate*, which was partially made in Wallace in 1979. The film is often cited among Hollywood's all-time biggest flops. But disaster movies, whether intentional or not, are nothing new in North Idaho: A silent film, *Tornado*, was filmed in the 1920s on the St. Joe River.

On the opposite end of the state, Preston, Idaho, found fame as the setting for the off-beat 2004 hit *Napoleon Dynamite*. Preston native Jared Hess made the independent film for $400,000; it earned $45 million in its first six months of theatrical release. (See the Southeastern Idaho chapter for more information on Napoleon's sweet success story.) Other films made entirely or partially in Idaho include Clint Eastwood's *Bronco Billy* and *Pale Rider*; *Northwest Passage* with Spencer Tracy; *Continental Divide*, with John Belushi in a tender-hearted role; *Smoke Signals*, written by Sherman Alexie; Nell Shipman's *Told in the Hills*; *River of No Return* with Marilyn Monroe; *Breakheart Pass*; *Sun Valley Serenade*; and *Dark Horse*, a family film about a troubled teenager's redemption. For information on filmmaking in Idaho, visit the Idaho Film Bureau's website at filmidaho.org or call (208) 334-2470.

in 1980; since then, the facility has been moved to accommodate the freeway and renovated to tell all about the Northern Pacific, which at one time boasted "2,000 miles of startling beauty." There is an extensive collection of Northern Pacific memorabilia, a model railroad display, and interactive exhibits.

The chateau-style Wallace depot has a fascinating history all its own. Built in 1901 with 15,000 bricks salvaged from what was to be a grand hotel in Tacoma, Washington, the station was visited two years later by then-president Theodore Roosevelt. It also has survived a string of near disasters: a 1906 flood, a 1910 fire that burned half of Wallace, and a 1914 runaway train that crashed only a few feet from the depot. The Northern Pacific Depot Railroad Museum is open daily from 9 a.m. to 5 p.m. Apr 15 through Oct 15. Suggested admission is $3.50 for adult or $8 per family. Call (208) 752-0111 or see npdepot.org for more information.

Last but certainly not least, the **Oasis Rooms Bordello Museum** at 605 Cedar St. documents another formerly important Wallace industry, one that thrived until near the end of the twentieth century. The Oasis Rooms were hardly unique; numerous brothels once stood along Wallace's main street, and prostitution was long an acceptable misdemeanor in the eyes of local law enforcement, especially because the town had about three times as many men as it did women. But in 1973, according to the *New York Times*, Democratic governor Cecil Andrus ordered that Wallace's brothels be shut down, possibly in response to an *Idaho Statesman* article in which Republican attorney Stanley Crow charged that Andrus had agreed to go easy on gambling and prostitution in North Idaho in return for a $25,000 campaign contribution. (Andrus denied the charge.) After the fuss subsided, the brothels quietly went back into business. But by the late 1980s, beset by the AIDS crisis and the faltering mining economy, only a few houses were left. The Oasis Rooms' employees would often make themselves scarce for a few days if FBI agents were rumored to be in town—and in January 1988, they left and never came back.

For that reason, the Oasis Rooms tour is a fascinating look at how these women worked and lived. The rooms are pretty much as the "girls" left them, with clothing, jewelry, and makeup strewn about. In the brothel's heyday, an employee might make $1,000 to $2,500 a week, and some women put themselves through college with their earnings. (The Oasis Rooms would not hire anyone from Wallace or the surrounding area.) But it's clear they worked hard for their money. A menu left on the wall when the Oasis Rooms closed revealed different services priced from $15 (for eight minutes of "straight, no frills") to $80 (for a bubble bath and an hour-long encounter). The madam kept 40 percent of all fees.

The Oasis Rooms Bordello Museum is open daily May through Sept from 10 a.m. to 5 p.m. The tour costs $5 per person. For more information call (208) 753-0801.

Photos from the past are displayed at the ***Beale House Bed and Breakfast,*** located 4 blocks from downtown in one of Wallace's most prominent old homes, a 1904 Colonial Revival. Hosts Jim and Linda See have collected pictures from their home's past owners, as well as from the University of Idaho's Barnard-Stockbridge Photographic Collection. Beale House has five guest rooms, one with a fireplace, another with a balcony, another with two full walls of windows. Room rates start at $225, including breakfast. There's also a spacious, fully furnished cottage available on the grounds, ideal for families or two couples traveling together. For more information or reservations, call (888) 752-7151.

East of Wallace, the ***Route of the Hiawatha*** mountain bike trail has stirred big excitement among cyclists. The 15-mile trail was built atop what was once the Milwaukee Road rail bed. Riders cross trestles (all with good guardrails) and pass through tunnels, including the 1.7-mile-long Taft Tunnel, which is why cyclists need to have a headlamp on their helmets. The mountain vistas are spectacular, and there's a fair chance you'll see wildlife. But the ride's biggest plus is that, with the help of a shuttle service, it's all downhill—actually a gentle grade of about 2 percent—making the Route of the Hiawatha a good choice for families. To get to the East Portal trailhead, where most people start, take I-90 over the Montana state line to exit 5 (Taft) and follow the signs. Trail day passes cost $10 per person, $6 for kids ages 6 to 13. The shuttle costs $9 for adults, $6 for children. The trail is open for riding or hiking late May through early October, and you can rent bikes (including the required helmets and lights) at Lookout Pass Ski and Recreation Area, located at I-90 exit 0 on the Idaho-Montana border. For more information see ridethehiawatha.com or call (208) 744-1301.

Nationally recognized outfitter ***Western Spirit Cycling*** offers a five-day, family-oriented cycling tour that takes in the Route of the Hiawatha and the Trail of the Coeur d'Alenes. The all-inclusive cost is $1,245 ($1,145 for children under age 14). For more info, see westernspirit.com or call (800) 845-2453.

From Wallace backtrack along I-90 to Highway 3, the ***White Pine Scenic Byway.*** This route leads through country crisscrossed by the St. Joe and St. Maries Rivers. The St. Joe in particular is interesting; at about 2,200 feet above sea level, it is reportedly the highest navigable river in the world. These days it's also gaining renown for its fly-fishing and challenging rapids.

The town of St. Maries (pronounced Saint Mary's) has a pair of town-and-country bed-and-breakfast options worth noting. Downtown at 1001

West Jefferson St., **Fort Hemenway Manor** was built in 1910 as the home of lumber baron Fred Hemenway. It offers an "elopement package" (starting at $600) complete with officiant, cake, flowers, champagne, and a night in the Hemenway Suite for people who seek a low-cost, high-style wedding with a few friends. Regular nightly room rates run from $85 to $275, including breakfast. For more information call (208) 245-7979 or see forthemenwaymanor.com.

Just outside of town, the **St. Joe Riverfront Bed & Breakfast** offers a more outdoorsy retreat. Cary and Val Day, who owned a travel agency in Spokane for many years, built the 3,700-square-foot home specifically as a bed-and-breakfast, and it shows. Lovely landscaped grounds and gardens meet 135 feet of riverfront, where guests have access to a beach and fire pit. Four guest rooms, each with private bath, reflect the family's wide travels; one, the Tuscan Room, has bright blues and yellows evocative of Italy, while the Vineyard Room decor features shades of plum, burgundy, and green. Room rates run $119 to $249, including breakfast. Ask about special interactive cooking weekends—in which guests enjoy dinners prepared around a culinary theme—and the ever-rollicking murder mystery parties. For more information or to make reservations, call (208) 245-8687 or visit stjoeriverbb.com.

South of St. Maries on Highway 3, you can pick up Highway 6 to continue on the White Pine Scenic Byway, or stay on Highway 3 to look for two great places to have fun and maybe pick up some unique Idaho souvenirs (if you don't mind getting your hands dirty). The star garnet is found in only two places in the world, Idaho and India. And in Idaho the best place to find these dark beauties is the **Emerald Creek Garnet Area** 6 miles west of Clarkia on Forest Road 447. Star garnets are so named because they have rays that seem to dance across the gem's purple- or plum-colored surface. There are usually four rays, but some gems—the most valuable kind—have six. In ancient times people believed garnets conferred a sense of calm and protection from wounds.

Garnets are typically found in alluvial deposits of gravel or sand just above bedrock, anywhere from 1 to 10 feet underground. The deposits along the East Fork of Emerald Creek are particularly rich. The Forest Service has developed a site where visitors can wash stockpiled gravel in sluice boxes to find garnets. You can get a permit at the sluice area, which is a half-mile hike from the parking lot. Permits are good for one day, and the cost is $10 for adults and $5 for children ages 6 to 12. Buckets, shovels, and special screen boxes are provided.

The garnet area is open from 9 a.m. to 4:30 p.m. Fri through Tues, Memorial Day weekend through Labor Day. Bring drinking water and snacks, sunscreen, a change of clothes, and a container for holding your garnets. Veteran garnet hunters say that lined rubber gloves, a small hammer and brush, and a collapsible stool are handy to have, too. Motorized equipment and pets are not allowed at the site. There is no shade in the parking lot, so it's best to leave pets at home.

The Idaho Panhandle National Forest offers the Emerald Creek and Cedar Creek campgrounds nearby. The closest motels are in St. Maries and Moscow. For more information call the Forest Service in St. Maries at (208) 245-2531 or search online for Emerald Creek Garnet Area.

Also near Clarkia is the locally famous *Fossil Bowl,* just south of town. This motorcycle racing track also serves as a prime fossil area with a world-class stash of fifteen-million-year-old leaves, as well as a few fossilized insects, fish, and flowers. For $10 per person (no charge for young children), anyone can dig at the site. The fossils are found by chopping blocks from the soft clay hillside, then prying apart the layers with a knife. Some undisturbed layers that have yet to be exposed to the elements can yield magnificent leaves in their original dark green or red—until the air turns them black, usually within a minute.

The Fossil Bowl still hosts motorcycle races on about a dozen days May through Oct, and anyone visiting on race days will get double for their entertainment dollar. The original fossil site is right by the racetrack, making for some dusty digging on race days, but another site farther from the commotion is now available as well. Digging is permitted daily except in winter, but it's best to call first to check on hours.

Visitors also may be interested in the Fossil Bowl's antiques collection, which includes century-old woodworking machinery. Although it's situated on Highway 3, the Fossil Bowl's legal address is Eighty-fifth and Plum—"85 miles out in the sticks and Plum the hell away from everything." For more information call (208) 245-3608 or visit fossilbowl.com.

Places to Stay in North Idaho

BONNERS FERRY

Best Western Plus Kootenai River Inn Casino & Spa
7169 Plaza St.
(888) 875-8259
kootenairiverinn.com
Moderate

Bonners Ferry Log Inn
Highway 95 North
(208) 267-3986
bonnersferryloginn.com
Inexpensive–Moderate

Northside School Bed & Breakfast
6497 Comanche St.
(208) 267-1826
northsideschoolbedand breakfast.com
Moderate

SANDPOINT

Best Western Edgewater Resort
56 Bridge St.
(800) 635-2534
bestwestern.com
Moderate–Expensive

Dover Bay Resort
651 Lakeshore (Dover)
(208) 263-5493
doverbaybungalows.com
Moderate–Expensive

Hotel Ruby Ponderay
477255 Highway 95 North
(Ponderay)
(208) 263-5383
hotelrubyponderay.com
Moderate

K2 Inn
501 North Fourth Ave.
(208) 263-3441
k2innsandpoint.com
Moderate–Expensive

LaQuinta Inn
415 Cedar St.
(800) 282-0660
laquintasandpoint.com
Moderate–Expensive

**Selkirk Lodge at
Schweitzer Mountain**
(877) 487-4643
schweitzer.com
Expensive

**Western Pleasure Guest
Ranch**
1413 Upper Gold Creek
Rd.
(888) 863-9066
westernpleasureranch.com
Moderate–Expensive

**PRIEST LAKE
(NORDMAN)**

Elkins Resort
404 Elkins Rd.
(208) 443-2432
elkinsresort.com
Moderate–Expensive
(Weekly rates in summer)

Hill's Resort
4777 West Lakeshore Rd.
(208) 443-2551
hillsresort.com
Moderate–Expensive

The Old Northern Inn
(208) 443-2426
oldnortherninn.com
Moderate

POST FALLS

**Red Lion Templin's
Hotel**
414 East First Ave.
(208) 773-1611
redlion.com/templins
Moderate

Riverbend Inn
4105 West Riverbend Ave.
(208) 773-3583
riverbend-inn.com
Moderate

Sleep Inn
157 South Pleasantview
Rd.
(208) 777-9394
choicehotels.com
Inexpensive–Moderate

HAYDEN

**Triple Play Resort Hotel
& Suites**
151 West Orchard Ave.
(208) 772-7900
tripleplayresort.com
Moderate–Expensive

COEUR D'ALENE

**Best Western Plus
Coeur d'Alene Inn**
506 West Appleway Ave.
(208) 765-3200
bestwestern.com
Moderate–Expensive

**Blackwell Boutique
Hotel**
820 East Sherman Ave.
(208) 765-7799
blackwellboutiquehotel
.com
Expensive

Coeur d'Alene Resort
115 South Second Ave.
(208) 765-4000
cdaresort.com
Moderate–Very Expensive

Flamingo Motel
718 Sherman Ave.
(208) 664-2159
Moderate

Roosevelt Inn
105 East Wallace Ave.
(800) 290-3358
therooseveltinn.com
Expensive–Very Expensive

Shilo Inn Suites Hotel
702 West Appleway Ave.
(208) 664-2300
shiloinns.com
Moderate

HARRISON

Osprey Inn
134 Frederick Ave.
(208) 689-9502
ospreybnb.com
Moderate

KELLOGG

**GuestHouse Inn
& Suites**
601 Bunker Ave.
(208) 783-1234
guesthouseintl.com
Moderate

**Morning Star Lodge at
Silver Mountain**
610 Bunker Ave.
(866) 344-2675
silvermt.com
Moderate–Expensive

Silverhorn Motor Inn
699 West Cameron Ave.
(208) 783-1151
Inexpensive–Moderate

WALLACE

**Beale House Bed and
Breakfast**
107 Cedar St.
(208) 752-7151
wallace-id.com/
bealehouse.html
Expensive

HELPFUL WEBSITES FOR NORTH IDAHO

North Idaho Visitor Information
visitnorthidaho.com

Idaho Spokesman-Review
spokesmanreview.com

Sandpoint Chamber of Commerce
sandpointchamber.com

Coeur d'Alene Press
cdapress.com

**Coeur d'Alene Visitor and
Convention Services**
coeurdalene.org

Wallace Inn
100 Front St.
(800) 643-2386
thewallaceinn.com
Moderate–Expensive

ST. MARIES

Fort Hemenway Manor
1001 West Jefferson Ave.
(208) 245-7979
forthemenwaymanor.com
Moderate–Expensive

The Pines Motel
1117 Main Ave.
(208) 245-2545
stmariesmotel.com
Inexpensive

**St. Joe Riverfront Bed
and Breakfast**
816 Shepherd Rd.
(208) 245-8687
stjoeriverbb.com
Moderate–Expensive

Places to Eat in
North Idaho

BONNERS FERRY

**Kootenai River Brewing
Company**
(brewpub)
6424 Riverside St.
(208) 267-4677
Moderate

Mi Pueblo
(Mexican)
7168 Main St.
(208) 267-4735
Inexpensive

Springs Restaurant
(American)
in the Kootenai River Inn
(208) 267-8511
Moderate

Under the Sun
(organic specialties)
7178 Main St.
(208) 267-6467
Inexpensive

SANDPOINT

Connie's Cafe
(American)
323 Cedar St.
(208) 255-2227
Inexpensive–Moderate

**Eichardt's Pub, Grill &
Coffee House**
(American)
212 Cedar St.
(208) 263-4005
Inexpensive–Moderate

Evans Brothers Coffee
(espresso and cafe)
524 Church St.
(208) 265-5553
Inexpensive

Fifth Avenue Restaurant
(family)
807 North Fifth Ave.
(208) 263-0596
Inexpensive–Moderate

Forty-one South
(Northwest)
41 Lakeshore Dr. (Sagle;
south end of the Long
Bridge)
(208) 265-2000
Moderate–Expensive

Hydra Steakhouse
(steak/seafood)
115 Lake St.
(208) 263-7123
Moderate–Expensive

Spuds Waterfront Grill
(American)
102 North First Ave.
(208) 265-4311
Inexpensive–Moderate

Trinity at City Beach
(Southern-inspired fare)
58 Bridge St.
(208) 255-7558
Moderate

HOPE

**Old Ice House Pizzeria
& Bakery**
140 West Main St.
(208) 264-5555
Inexpensive–Moderate

DOVER

Dish at Dover Bay Cafe
(American)
Lakeshore Avenue
Dover Bay Resort
(208) 265-6467
Moderate

PRIEST LAKE

Elkins Resort
(American)
40 Elkins Rd.
(208) 443-2432
Moderate–Expensive

Hill's Resort
(American)
4777 West Lakeshore Rd.
(208) 443-2551
Moderate–Expensive

SPIRIT LAKE

**White Horse Saloon,
Hotel & Cafe**
(American)
6248 West Maine St.
(208) 623-2353
Inexpensive–Moderate

HAUSER LAKE

Embers by the Lake
(upscale pizza)
12008 Woodland Beach
Dr.
(208) 262-8219
Moderate

POST FALLS

Famous Willie's BBQ
(Southern)
107 East Seventh Ave.
(200) 773-0000
Moderate

Fleur de Sel
(European)
4365 Inverness Dr.
(208) 777-7600
Moderate–Expensive

White House Grill
(Mediterranean)
712 North Spokane St.
(208) 777-9672
Moderate

COEUR D'ALENE

**Adventures in
Deliciousness**
(food truck)
3033 North Government
Way
(208) 755-3446
Inexpensive

Beverly's
(fine dining)
in the Coeur d'Alene
Resort
(208) 765-4000
Expensive

**Cedars Floating
Restaurant**
(seafood)
1514 North Marina Dr.
(off US 95 south of town)
(208) 664-2922
Expensive

The Cellar
(fine dining)
317 Sherman Ave.
(208) 664-9463
Moderate–Expensive

**Crafted Tap House
& Kitchen**
(Northwest)
523 Sherman Ave.
(208) 292-4813
Inexpensive–Moderate

Hudson's Hamburgers
(American)
207 East Sherman Ave.
(208) 664-5444
Inexpensive

Java on Sherman
(coffeehouse)
819 East Sherman Ave.
(208) 667-0010
Inexpensive

ALSO WORTH SEEING IN NORTH IDAHO

Brooks Seaplane
Coeur d'Alene

Heyburn State Park
Plummer

Coeur d'Alene Casino
Worley

Silver Streak Zipline Tours
Wallace

Crystal Gold Mine
Kellogg

Moon Time
(casual pub)
1602 Sherman Ave.
(208) 667-2331
Inexpensive–Moderate

Wolf Lodge Inn
(steakhouse)
I-90 exit 22, east of Coeur d'Alene
(208) 664-6665
Expensive

KINGSTON

The Snake Pit
(family)
I-90 exit 43
(208) 682-3453
Moderate

KELLOGG

Humdinger Drive-In
(American)
205 North Hill St.
(208) 786-7395
Inexpensive

Moose Creek Grill
(American)
12 Emerson Lane
(208) 783-2625
Moderate

WALLACE

Albi's Steakhouse
(American)
Sixth and Pine Streets
(208) 753-3071
Moderate

Red Light Garage
(American)
302 Fifth St.
(208) 556-0575
Inexpensive

1313 Club
(American)
608 Bank St.
(208) 752-9391
Inexpensive–Moderate

ST. MARIES

Bud's Drive-In
(burgers)
101 West College Ave.
(208) 245-3312
Inexpensive

Pizza Factory
910 Main St.
(208) 245-5515
Inexpensive

North Central Idaho

In Idaho, geography has decreed that there are simply some places where roads cannot go—or where travelers can pass only with much effort. In North Central Idaho, nature makes the rules and humans play along as well as we're able. There is only one east–west road, US 12, across this region—and it was not completed until 1962. The major north–south route, US 95, also evolved according to geography.

It's 196 miles from Moscow to McCall, but you're not going to make this trip in four hours. Between long hill climbs and river-hugging curves, it's slow, scenic going wherever you travel in North Central Idaho. The main routes are alluring enough, but plan to explore some of the secondary roads, too. The Lolo Highway, the Elk City Wagon Road, the Magruder Road, and the climb to the Hells Canyon Rim at Heaven's Gate are just a few of this region's many great byways.

For more North Central Idaho travel information, call (208) 507-1904 or see visitnorthcentralidaho.org.

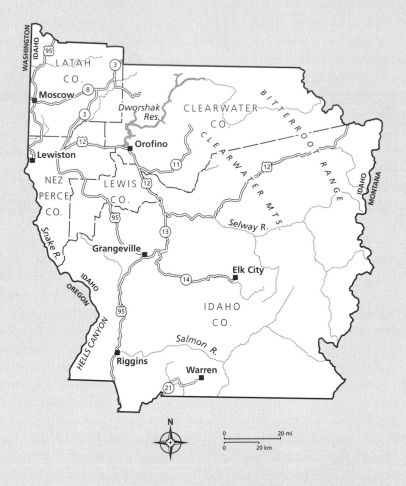

Palouse and Clearwater Country

North Central Idaho is a land of contrast, and nowhere is this fact more visible than in Latah and Clearwater Counties, where rolling farmlands seamlessly give way to dense forests. This is the Palouse (pronounced "pah-LOOSE"), a rich agricultural region that spills across the Idaho-Washington border. You can get a good sense of the terrain by turning off just about any side road from US 95, but there are few better places to start a tour of the area than *Mary Minerva McCroskey State Park.*

Although it's among Idaho's largest and oldest state parks, McCroskey is also one of the state's most forgotten. Virgil T. McCroskey grew up looking at this ridge from his boyhood home at the base of Steptoe Butte, just over the Washington state line. He later bought the land, turned it into a parkway in honor of his mother, and sought to donate it to the state of Idaho. The state wasn't too interested, but it finally took charge after McCroskey agreed to put up money for maintenance until his death. Since then, the park has remained undeveloped, but its 18-mile Skyline Drive and 32 miles of trails afford many good views of the Palouse. To get there, drive 25 miles north of Moscow via US 95 and watch for the Skyline Drive sign atop a hill not far north of the state rest area. Turn west (which is left, if you're heading north), and follow the road through thick pine forests into the preserve. You'll find a few picnic areas and primitive campsites scattered along the drive. The road isn't recommended for vehicles of more than 28 feet in length. See parksandrecreation.idaho.gov/parks/mccroskey for maps and more info.

Another short detour from US 95 on Highway 6 leads to the small town of Potlatch. The city's Scenic 6 Historical Park has RV and tent camping, plus a walking trail, disc golf, and a playground. Nearby, the old Washington, Idaho & Montana rail station is home to *BlackBird at the Depot.* Open Wed afternoons

AUTHOR'S FAVORITES IN NORTH CENTRAL IDAHO

Shattuck Arboretum
Moscow

Lolo Motorway
north of US 12

Nez Perce National Historical Park
region-wide

Wolf Education and Research Center
Winchester

Dog Bark Park
Cottonwood

Heaven's Gate
west of Riggins

Dig This

Idaho is not the first place that comes to mind when you think about jazz. So fans of America's indigenous music are pleasantly surprised to learn that Idaho has a rich jazz scene. In Moscow, the University of Idaho is the setting for the annual *Lionel Hampton International Jazz Festival,* one of the premier events of its kind. Held during the last weekend in February, the festival has recently featured Dianne Reeves, Stefon Harris, Tower of Power, and dozens of other top jazz stars. Leonard Feather, the late jazz critic for the *Los Angeles Times,* once called it "the number one jazz festival in the world." The festival also serves as a workshop for thousands of music students who travel to Moscow to play with the pros. For ticket and schedule information, call (208) 885-5900 or see uidaho.edu/class/jazzfest.

and Thurs through Sat from 9 a.m. to 4 p.m., this cool little shop has fun gifts plus Idaho-inspired art by owner Karen Rohn, who also takes her wares to craft fairs throughout the region in a little black trailer. See more at karenrohn.com.

Moscow, home to the University of Idaho, took its name not from the city in Russia but from a community in Pennsylvania. In its early years, Moscow had an even more unusual name: Hog Heaven, so called because farmers saw their pigs munching merrily on the camas bulbs so prevalent in the area. In 1889 Moscow was named the site of Idaho's federal land-grant college. It may seem odd that the state's namesake university is so far from Idaho's population center in Boise, but despite or perhaps even because of its remoteness, Moscow is a quintessential college town—a blend of funky charm and high-tech attitude and more liberal than anywhere else in the state, with the exception of Boise and Sun Valley/Ketchum.

The U of I is blessed with a beautiful campus that includes the nineteen-acre **Shattuck Arboretum,** one of the oldest university arboretums in the western United States. Planted from 1910 to 1917, the arboretum is a pleasant place for a stroll amid native Idaho trees, as well as those introduced from other regions. Just across Nez Perce Drive from Shattuck Arboretum, the sixty-three-acre University of Idaho Arboretum and Botanical Garden was planted during the 1980s. It showcases trees and shrubs from around the world grouped by their geographical origin. For self-guiding brochures to both arboretums, visit the campus information center on Pullman Road (Highway 8) and Line Street. Guided tours may be arranged by calling (208) 885-6250.

Idaho's state horse, the Appaloosa, is best known by the spots on its rump. Learn everything you ever wanted to know about Appaloosas and more at the **Appaloosa Museum** in Moscow. Exhibits recount the evolution of the Appaloosa, historical aspects of the breed, and its importance to the Nez Perce

TOP ANNUAL EVENTS IN NORTH CENTRAL IDAHO

Lionel Hampton Jazz Festival
Moscow (late Feb)

Dogwood Festival
Lewiston (late Apr)

Renaissance Fair
Moscow (early May)

Avista-NAIA World Series
Lewiston (late May)

Border Days
Grangeville (early July)

Chief Looking Glass Pow Wow
Kamiah (mid-Aug)

Lumberjack Days
Orofino (mid-Sept)

Indians. In the summer months you'll find a picnic area with horses grazing nearby. The museum is on Moscow's western edge at 2720 West Pullman Rd., and it's open from 11 a.m. to 4 p.m. Mon through Thurs, 10:30 a.m. to 4 p.m. Fri, and 10 a.m. to 4 p.m. Sat year-round. Suggested donation is $3 per adult, $1 per child, or $5 per family. Call (208) 882-5578 or see appaloosamuseum .org for more information.

Moscow's downtown is a delightful spot to wander around a while. *Prichard Art Gallery* at 414 South Main St. is affiliated with the University of Idaho and has free admission and a neat gift shop. *The Storm Cellar* at 504 South Main is a huge consignment shop with loads of vintage clothing and housewares. First-run films, live performances, and summer Saturday morning cartoons are on the bill at the *Kenworthy Performing Arts Centre* at 508 South Main. See kenworthy.org for a calendar. *BookPeople,* one of Idaho's best independent bookstores, is at 521 South Main, while *Bloom* is a hot spot for breakfast and lunch, with outdoor seating at 403 South Main on a pedestrian plaza known as Friendship Square. The plaza also is the site of a longtime farmers' market that takes place every Sat morning May through Oct.

Elk River, at the tail end of Highway 8 east of Moscow, serves as the north gateway to *Dworshak Reservoir.* It's a great place to camp, pick huckleberries, fish, hunt, snowmobile, cross-country ski, and enjoy the Idaho outdoors. The *Elk River Lodge & General Store* has rooms priced from $55 to $115. Most share bathroom facilities, but two (the Elk Suite and the Loft Room) have private bathrooms. Call (208) 826-3299 or see elkriverlodge.net for information.

Before you leave Elk River, take a walk around town. It's the kind of place where every family has its members' names posted on the welcome sign. There's also a handsome old schoolhouse built in 1912, perched on a hill over-

Pedaling the Palouse

If you'd like to see the Palouse under your own power, several connecting trails offer opportunities for biking, walking, and even cross-country skiing when the weather permits. The *Bill Chipman Palouse Trail* is a paved 8-mile path that runs from Moscow west to the neighboring college town of Pullman, Washington. The *Latah Trail* is paved for 12 miles between Moscow and Troy, Idaho, and the two are linked by the 2-mile Paradise Path through Moscow. *Paradise Creek Bicycles* at 513 South Main in Moscow offers hourly, daily, and weekly bike rentals as well as advice on places to ride throughout the region.

looking the town. It's no longer used, but a nearby church built the same year is still in operation. For a more vigorous workout, consider a hike up 5,824-foot *Elk Butte,* where a panoramic view awaits all who make it to the top.

Several other natural attractions are within easy drives of Elk River. Just west of town *Elk Creek Falls*—actually three separate falls—are reached via a set of short trails that run along what was once the old route to Orofino. If you have time to visit only one of the cascades, make it Middle Falls, at 90 feet the highest of the three. Along the way hikers pass the site of Elk Creek Falls School, which operated between 1910 and 1930. The forest has reclaimed the building, but its gateposts still stand.

Some of Idaho's oldest and tallest trees may be seen north of Elk River. The paved and accessible *Giant Red Cedar National Recreation Trail* (Trail 748) leads to a 177-foot-tall tree that's more than 18 feet in diameter and more than 3,000 years old. From Elk River, drive 10 miles north on County Road 382, then turn right on Forest Road 4764.

The Dent Road leads from Elk River to Dworshak Dam and Reservoir. *Dworshak Dam,* about 5 miles from Orofino, is notable because at 717 feet tall, it's the highest straight-axis, concrete gravity dam in the Western world and the largest ever built by the US Army Corps of Engineers. A visitor center overlooks the dam; call (800) 321-3198 to check hours. US 12 west and southeast of Orofino is known as the *Northwest Passage Scenic Byway,* and it's here where the velvety brown hillsides of the Inland Northwest meet the mountains and forests of the Rockies, sometimes intercepted by vast plateaus and prairies. Take Highway 11 east of Greer for a scenic drive across this changing landscape.

From Greer the highway climbs a dizzying grade onto the Weippe Prairie. It's about 12 miles from the town of Weippe to Pierce, site of the *Pierce Courthouse,* the first government building in Idaho. The Pierce area boomed in the early 1860s after the discovery of gold, and the courthouse was built in 1862 to serve what was then Shoshone County, Washington Territory. (The Idaho Territory was established a year later, and Pierce is now in Clearwater County.) The mining boom led to the 1863 redrawing of Nez Perce reservation boundaries to exclude Pierce and other areas of mineral wealth. As a result, the Nez Perce were left with a reservation that was a tenth the size they'd agreed to just eight years before. The courthouse and nearby *Bradbury Logging Museum* are generally open from noon to 4 p.m. Fri and Sat mid-June through Labor Day and Sat only through mid-Oct. From Pierce, travelers can retrace their route back to Weippe or continue north to Headquarters, Idaho, and the North Fork Adventure Road, a backcountry route to Superior, Montana.

Weippe can also be a jumping-off spot for the Lolo Trail, the famous path trod first by Native Americans and later by Lewis and Clark on their trek across the continent. It was just outside Weippe, in fact, that the Corps of Discovery (as President Thomas Jefferson dubbed the Lewis and Clark party) met the Nez Perce, who were to become indispensable to the white men's survival. Murals and exhibits at the *Weippe Discovery Center* at 204 Wood St. in Weippe detail the encounter. The center doubles as the town library and visitor center and is open daily except Sun, but the exterior murals are visible all the time.

The Lolo Trail

Lewis and Clark had been told the Lolo Trail crossing could be made in five days, but it took the corps twice that time, and they almost froze and starved en route. An early snow blanketed the mountains, and—with no game to be found—the explorers were reduced to eating horse meat and candle wax. Finally, on September 20, 1805, Clark and an advance party of six other men dragged themselves out of the Bitterroot Mountains and onto the Weippe Prairie. Their route over the mountains can still be traced over the Lolo Motorway, accessible from the west via Weippe or Kamiah, or from the east via Forest Roads 569 (Parachute Hill) or 107 north from US 12. The *Lolo Motorway*—also known as Forest Road 500—is one of the roughest roads you'll encounter anywhere, but for history buffs, it's well worth the time and effort it takes to travel. The route is usually accessible only from mid-July through mid-Sept. Four-wheel drive isn't a must, but a vehicle with good clearance is essential. For updated information, contact the Nez Perce–Clearwater National Forest's ranger stations in Kooskia at (208) 926-4274 or Powell at (208) 942-3113.

Castle Butte Lookout, a former working fire tower situated near the motorway, is a wonderful place to get away from civilization for a while. The lookout is about 15 feet square and is perched on a stone foundation about 20 feet high. Visitors are treated to sweeping views in all directions, but especially to the south, where the Selway-Bitterroot Wilderness stretches beyond the Lochsa River and east into Montana. The river itself is barely visible thousands of feet below this ridge.

Castle Butte Lookout can accommodate four people in two twin beds and two cots. There's also a propane cook stove, lights, and heater, but you need to bring your own water and bedding. It's a great place to read, write, nap, and daydream. Visitors also can amuse themselves by learning to use the firefinder (a device consisting of a map and a sighting instrument used to determine the location of a forest fire), exploring the local terrain, or rummaging through artifacts left by previous lookout tenants: a copy of *The Smokechaser,* a memoir by former fire lookout Carl A. Weholt; a deck of playing cards; and old magazines. The lookout is available for rent from mid- to late summer. Book online at recreation.gov.

Several Lolo Trail landmarks are a short hike or drive from Castle Butte. To the east are the Sinque Hole, where Lewis and Clark camped September 17, 1805, and the Smoking Place, where the returning explorers stopped in June 1806 to share a pipe with their Nez Perce guides. To the west, the dry camp of September 18, 1805, was where Captain Clark moved ahead with six hunters to look for game. And from nearby Sherman Peak, the captains first glimpsed the distant prairies. The corps called this spot Spirit Revival Ridge, realizing that their toilsome mountain travel was almost behind them.

US 12, the modern road paralleling the explorers' route, provides many interesting sights of its own. Traveling from east to west, Lolo Pass is on the Montana-Idaho state line. The ***Packer Meadows*** near here is especially beautiful in mid-June when the purple camas are in bloom, but it's also an excellent spot for cross-country skiing. The picnic area near milepost 165 on US 12 is known as the ***DeVoto Memorial Cedar Grove,*** named in honor of Bernard DeVoto, a noted writer and historian. Western red cedars tower here over the spot where DeVoto often camped while editing the Lewis and Clark journals, well before US 12 was completed in 1961. DeVoto's ashes were sprinkled over the grove after his death in 1955.

Powell, a little outpost along the highway, is the last place to buy gas until Lowell, about 50 miles west. The ***Lochsa Lodge*** has been feeding and lodging travelers since 1929, with accommodations ranging from rustic cabins with shared bathrooms for about $75 to $105 a night plus fancier cabins and rooms starting at $110. Horseback trail rides are available July through Sept, and snowshoeing gear can be reserved in winter. Call (208) 942-3405 or visit lochsalodge.com for updated rates and information.

Colgate Licks and ***Jerry Johnson Hot Springs,*** both located near US 12 west of the Wendover-Whitehouse campgrounds, are among the most popular stops along the highway. At Colgate Licks deer, elk, and other animals are attracted by the springs' saltiness. Take the loop trail from the parking lot to reach the springs. The Jerry Johnson site is accessed by a mile-long trail up Warm Springs Creek. The **Lochsa Historical Ranger Station,** with one of the West's best collections of Forest Service memorabilia, is also worth a stop. It's located across from the Wilderness Gateway campground, among the most pleasant along US 12.

At Lowell, Idaho, the Lochsa and Selway Rivers meet to form the Middle Fork of the Clearwater River. This is an area well-known to the folks at ROW Adventures, who've been offering river trips here and across Idaho and beyond since 1979. ROW operates the **River Dance Lodge** a few miles down Highway 12, in the hamlet of Syringa. Handcrafted log cabins sleep four to ten people. Each has its own front deck and hot tub. Rates start at $259 June through early Sept, with discounts available in spring and fall. Luxury camping tents have real beds and a private back porch with a propane-heated bathtub for $129 in summer, and budget tent camping is available, too, for $9 per person per night, including access to showers. In summer, River Dance becomes a base for all-inclusive family adventure camps that feature raft and kayak trips, fishing, mountain biking, and more. River Dance also runs the long-beloved Syringa Cafe, which serves globally inspired dishes as well as traditional Idaho fare. For more information or reservations, see riverdance lodge.com or call (866) 769-8747.

Travelers looking for the hospitality of a bed-and-breakfast combined with the privacy of a motel will enjoy staying at **Reflections Inn,** one of the most restful, friendly accommodations in North Central Idaho. The one-

Lolo Trail Area Tours

Whether you're interested in horseback riding, mountain biking, hiking, or interpreted scenic drives, guided tours are a good way to experience Lewis and Clark history in North Central Idaho. Much of the country here is wild and remote, and guides can ensure you have a safe, trouble-free trip.

Horseback riding specialists include Triple "O" Outfitters, (513) 254-1261, triple-o-out fitters.com, and Weitas Creek Outfitters, (888) 983-WEST, idahooutfitter.com. Lewis & Clark Trail Adventures holds a commemorative five-day hiking trip each September on the exact dates the expedition traveled. See specialty trips at trailadventures.com for details and call (800) 366-6246 for reservations. Odyssey Tours, (208) 791-8721, odytours.net, is an Idaho-based company that includes winter book retreats at the Lochsa Lodge and Lolo Trail treks among its far-flung tours with noted humanities scholar Clay Jenkinson.

time guest ranch is perched on a hillside above the Clearwater River about 11 miles east of Kooskia. Each of the eight rooms has its own entrance and bathroom and is individually decorated in casually elegant style. A communal kitchen/family room makes this a good spot for reunions and small-group retreats. Outside there's a barbecue grill, hot tub, and ten wooded acres to explore. High-season rates mid-May through Sept start at $125 per room, including a gourmet breakfast, for two people. For more information call (208) 926-0855 or see reflectionsinn.com.

Land of the Nez Perce

The Nez Perce people—or Nimi'ipuu ("we the people"), as they call them-selves—have played a substantial role in the history of what is now Idaho, as well as that of the United States as a whole. For more than a century, history students have been moved by the words of Nez Perce leader Chief Joseph who, upon his tribe's capture in Montana, made his famous "I will fight no more forever . . ." speech. Those words, uttered just 42 miles short of refuge at the Canadian border, marked the end of a 1,000-mile march punctuated by the battles of the Nez Perce War.

The war was precipitated by the discovery of gold on the Nez Perce reser-vation, which—by the original treaty signed in 1855—included most of the tribe's traditional homeland. When the gold was found, however, the US government redrew the reservation's boundaries to exclude the areas of mineral wealth. One Nez Perce leader known as Lawyer accepted the new boundaries and signed a new treaty. But other members of the tribe, led by Old Joseph, did not agree, and soon there were two bands of Nez Perce: the "treaty" and "nontreaty."

Soon after Lawyer signed the treaty in 1867, the government launched a campaign to move all Nez Perce to the new reservation. The nontreaty Nez Perce ignored the government's orders, and for a time they were able to live peaceably. But by 1877 the government was ready to force the nontreaty Nez Perce to move, and a June 14 deadline was set.

In the meantime Young Joseph had succeeded his father. He did not wish to move, nor did he wish to wage war, so he moved his followers toward the reservation. Before they made it, however, three young Nez Perce men—angry at the forced move and seeking revenge for the death of one of their fathers—killed four white settlers by noon on June 14. Over the next few days, other Nez Perce joined in and an additional fourteen or fifteen whites were slain. The Nez Perce War was on.

Although the Nez Perce trail crosses through several states, North Central Idaho and adjacent areas in Oregon and Washington make up the tribe's ancestral homeland. For that reason the ***Nez Perce National Historical Park*** was established in the Gem State. Unlike most national park sites, however, the Nez Perce park isn't one specific place. Instead it includes thirty-eight sites scattered across this region. Two of the most interesting are located near US 12 between Kamiah and Lewiston.

Just outside Kamiah, a basaltic formation known as the ***Heart of the Monster*** explains how the Nez Perce came to be. According to tribal legend, Coyote—a mythical figure central to much Native American literature—killed a great monster near here. The Nez Perce and other tribes were created, each as parts of the monster fell to the earth. An audio station at the site retells the legend, first in the Nez Perce's native tongue, then in English. Kamiah is also the site of the annual Chief Looking Glass Pow Wow held the third weekend of August. This traditional gathering features descendants of Chief Looking Glass, a Nez Perce leader, participating in dancing and other cultural activities.

The Nez Perce National Historical Park headquarters are at Spalding, east of Lewiston on US 95. This is where Henry and Eliza Spalding established their mission to the Nez Perce in the 1830s. A Presbyterian missionary, Spalding believed it was his duty to Christianize the Indians. "What is done for the poor Indians of this Western world must be done soon," he said. "The only thing that can save them from annihilation is the introduction of civilization."

The ***Spalding Site,*** as the headquarters are sometimes called, features an excellent visitor center that catalogs the changes—both good and bad—this philosophy wrought for the Nez Perce. Exhibits include a *Book of Matthew* printed in the Nez Perce language, a case full of beautiful beadwork, and a silk ribbon and silver friendship medal presented to the Nez Perce by Lewis and Clark. Another highlight is a 32-foot canoe made in 1837 from a single cottonwood log. The visitor center is open daily from 8 a.m. to 5 p.m. from late May through Labor Day and 8 a.m. to 4:30 p.m. the rest of the year. For more information on the park and its sites, see nps.gov/nepe.

Lewiston is the largest city in North Central Idaho, and it has more than 15 miles of trails for joggers, cyclists, walkers, and strollers. Many of these paths are on the Lewiston Levee, which was constructed by the US Army Corps of Engineers to protect Lewiston after the completion of Lower Granite Dam down the Snake River.

At the west end of Lewiston's charming downtown, ***Morgan's Alley*** at 301 Main St. is a collection of specialty shops and restaurants. The "alley" is actually four old buildings linked together by thirteen stairways and seventeen brick arches. Interspersed among the Alley's shops are numerous artifacts from area history. An old-fashioned gas pump marks the entrance to ***Bojacks,*** a steak-and-seafood eatery and cocktail lounge open since the 1950s. Sets of doors came from the local sheriff's office and the Lewiston National Bank. And so on. In fine weather, you might see a piano on the sidewalk bookended by the head and tail of an elephant. This (and a plaque across the street) commemorates the story of Mary, a circus elephant who sadly met her untimely demise in August 1928 when cornered while trying to find a drink of water. Yes, it's OK to play the piano. Morgan's Alley also is a meeting spot for ninety-minute guided walking tours of downtown Lewiston offered by historian Garry Bush, who also leads trolley tours of Lewiston's Normal Hill neighborhood and an occasional wine tour, too. See idahohistorytours.com for dates and details.

The Blue Lantern at 326 Main St. is a hub in one of downtown's loveliest old buildings, a wonderful spot for morning coffee and pastries or a late-afternoon glass of local wine or craft beer. It's usually closed by dinnertime, but Wednesday is knitter's night until 8 p.m. and old-time music jam sessions take place the third Thursday of many months. Check the business's Facebook page for updates.

Lewis-Clark State College runs the *LCSC Center for Arts & History* at 415 Main St., with regular special exhibits and events. Its gallery is open from 11 a.m. to 4 p.m. Tues through Sat. Local history is also the focus at the *Nez Perce County Museum,* at Third and C Streets. The museum sits on the site occupied by one of Lewiston's first buildings, the Luna House Hotel. After serving as a hotel, the building also functioned as a courthouse for a few years in the late 1880s. Today's museum is home to a collection of Nez Perce and pioneer artifacts, along with a striking trio of paintings by Dan Piel portraying the Nez Perce leader Chief Joseph in his youth, maturity, and old age. The museum is open from 10 a.m. to 4 p.m. Tues through Sat, Mar through mid-Dec. Admission is $4 for adults and $2 for students ages 11 to 17. Younger children get in free. Call (208) 743-2535 for more information.

Lewiston spends much of the month of April celebrating the arrival of spring with the annual *Dogwood Festival,* named for the hundreds of dogwood trees and perennial plants that burst forth in bloom that time of year. Events typically include Art Under the Elms, an outdoor art festival on the LCSC campus; the Confluence Grape & Grain microbrew and wine festival; a quilt show; a dog show; a fun run; and a concert. Get a calendar of events at lcsc.edu/ce/dogwood. Over Memorial Day weekend, the town plays host to the *National Association of Intercollegiate Athletics' Baseball World Series* at Harris Field on the LCSC campus. It's a good chance to catch some future baseball stars from leading small-college programs. See naiaworldseries .com for information.

Lewiston is the northern gateway for *Hells Canyon,* the deepest river-carved gorge in the Northwest. *Hells Gate State Park* offers close-to-town

Do the Twist

For a different perspective on Lewiston and environs, check out the famous *Spiral Highway* north of town. This twisting road with sixty-four curves climbs 2,000 feet to the top of Lewiston Hill. It was completed in 1917 at a cost of $100,000—about twice the projected tab. Until 1979 the Spiral Highway was the only route from Lewiston to the Palouse region above. It's still open to traffic, but most motorists now use the newer four-lane section of US 95. Either way, stop at the overlook at the top of the hill for a great view of Lewiston, neighboring Clarkston, Washington, the confluence of the Clearwater and Snake Rivers, and the rolling farmland all around.

camping plus kayak rentals, hiking trails, Lewis and Clark interpretive displays, and a Hunting Heritage & Education Center showcasing memorabilia from *Outdoor Life* journalist Jack O'Connor. Get more information at parksandrecreation .idaho.gov/parks/hells-gate.

Hells Canyon National Recreation Area straddles the Snake River south of Lewiston and includes parts of Oregon's Wallowa-Whitman National Forest and the Nez Perce and Payette National Forests of Idaho. Many outfitters offer jet boat or rafting trips through the canyon. For a list search online for Hells Canyon Wild and Scenic Snake River. Among them, **Snake River Adventures** and **Adventures Afloat** offer overnight lodging and meals within the canyon.

Private rafters and jet-boaters also may travel the river, but a Forest Service permit is required before launching. River trips also leave from the canyon's south end at Hells Canyon Dam northwest of Cambridge, Idaho; see the Southwestern Idaho chapter for more details on those.

Just outside Winchester, the Wolf Education and Research Center includes a twenty-acre enclosure that is home to a small pack of wolves that serve as ambassadors for their wild cousins who were reintroduced in Idaho and elsewhere in the Rocky Mountain region. The center was originally home to a pack of wolves from the Sawtooth Mountains north of Sun Valley. It's now a sanctuary for several wolves that federal authorities confiscated from a backyard near Murphy, Idaho, where WERC says they'd been housed in small enclosures and fed inadequate diets.

The center is open daily Memorial Day weekend through Labor Day weekend. For a suggested donation of $5 ($2 for children ages 6 to 12), visitors can take a self-guided tour anytime between 9 a.m. and 5 p.m. Also available are naturalist-guided tours led by a member of the center staff. Because early mornings or evenings are the best times to see wolves and hear them howl, these tours are scheduled most summer days at 7:30 a.m. and 7 p.m. The cost is $10 for adults and kids 12 and older; $4 for younger children with a paying adult. For more information or to book a tour, visit wolfcenter.org.

The wolf center is near ***Winchester State Park,*** a popular place for camping and fishing in summer and cross-country skiing, ice fishing, and ice-skating in winter. The park has four yurts available for rent year-round. Equipped with electricity and heat and big enough to sleep five, the yurts cost $50 to $70 per night. They can be reserved by calling (888) 922-6743 or visiting parksandrec reation.idaho.gov/parks/winchester.

South of the Nez Perce reservation border on US 95, near the town of Cottonwood, you can't miss the sight of Sweet Willy, a 30-foot-high beagle looming over ***Dog Bark Park.*** Look closer and you'll see Sweet Willy actually doubles as a guest house that can comfortably sleep a family of four. The "doghouse" has a queen bed, small kitchen, and bathroom in the main quarters and a loft with two twin futons up in the pup's head. Sweet Willy is available Apr through Oct for $92 a night for one person or $98 double occupancy; $10 each for extra people; well-behaved pets $15 on advance approval. Overnight accommodations include an extensive continental breakfast with tasty granola, homemade pastries, yogurt, hard-boiled eggs, and more. There's air-conditioning, Wi-Fi, and board games to play, but no TV. For more information or a reservation, call (208) 962-3647 or see dogbark parkinn.com. This clever idea was the brainchild of Dennis J. Sullivan, who with his wife, Frances Conklin, had already found some measure of fame as chain saw artists specializing in dogs. A gift shop featuring their work is open year-round from 11 a.m. to 4 p.m. There's also a picnic area and information center for passersby, along with a restroom for visitors. (Look for the 10-foot-high fire hydrant!)

Also near Cottonwood, the ***Monastery of St. Gertrude*** sits high on a hill overlooking the Camas Prairie. The monastery is well worth a visit for its stone chapel, an impressive museum, and restful accommodations. St. Gertrude's Chapel was built in 1924 of blue porphyry stone quarried nearby. Each stone was individually chiseled and placed by hand, with the nuns themselves doing much of the work. The resulting Romanesque structure and its 97-foot twin towers may be seen for miles around. The tower's bells are rung daily to call the Benedictine sisters of St. Gertrude's to prayer or to Mass, but they're also sounded at times of severe storms as a prayer for protection. The chapel's interior is equally striking, most notably the German altar at the front. In deference to the pain Jesus Christ felt when he was hung on the cross, not one nail was used to make the altar; each part was mortised and glued. A self-guiding tour brochure is available inside the chapel.

The St. Gertrude community welcomes overnight visitors in two ways. Its Spirit Center offers a variety of organized, themed retreats as well as individual stays for rest and renewal. The Inn at St. Gertrude is a more traditional bed-and-breakfast experience, offering hospitality in the Benedictine tradition. See stgertrudes.org for a calendar of events and other information.

The Historical Museum at St. Gertrude is also worth a visit, particularly for the collection of Samuel Emmanuel, who gave the museum a treasure trove of artistic pieces ranging from Ming ceramics to a French cabinet that appeared in the 1896 World's Fair in Chicago to a Czechoslovakian chandelier bedecked with more than 1,000 crystals. This European finery may seem out of place on the prairies of Idaho, but plenty of local lore is represented, too, most notably an exhibit about the life of Polly Bemis. Having been sold into slavery as a young girl in China, this fascinating woman was 19 years old when she arrived in the Warren mining camps of Idaho. She wound up marrying saloonkeeper Charlie Bemis and running a boardinghouse.

The **Historical Museum at St. Gertrude** is open 9:30 a.m. to 4:30 p.m. Tues through Sat year-round. Admission is $6 for adults and $3 for children ages 7 to 17. The museum holds an annual Raspberry Festival the first Sun of Aug. This popular fund-raiser has food, live music, a craft show, and more. For additional information or to arrange a group tour, call (208) 962-2050 or see historicalmuseumatstgertrude.org. A few scenic miles west of the museum and monastery, **Keuterville Pub and Grub** is a rustic saloon and eatery that's regionally famous for its all-you-can-eat Taco Tuesdays.

At the north entrance of Grangeville, it's worth a brief stop to check out the **mammoth exhibit** in Eimer's Park. In 1994 a heavy-equipment operator working at the bed of Tolo Lake 6 miles west of Grangeville discovered what turned out the be the thigh bone of a male Columbian mammoth. The Idaho Museum of Natural History from Pocatello led digs at the site in the summer of 1995 and found bones from at least nine mammoths. The glassed-in pavilion here in Grangeville features a full-size mammoth replica, as well as a mural by local artist Robert Thomas depicting what the Tolo Lake area may have looked like about 12,000 years ago when mammoths were on the scene. Tolo Lake, meanwhile, has refilled and is a popular spot for fishing and birdwatching.

When Grangeville got going back in 1876, the Grange Hall was the first building in town, which is how the city got its name. The hall later fell to fire, but a new building went up in 1909 and still stands on the northeast corner of Main and Hall Streets. It is now home to **Oscar's Restaurant,** one of the region's best. This is the place for a hearty breakfast or a satisfying sandwich for lunch. Dinner choices include steak, prime rib, seafood, and chicken, with

The Deepest Canyon?

Name the deepest gorge in North America. In Idaho, you'll frequently hear the claim that the obvious choice—the Grand Canyon—is not it and that Hells Canyon on the Idaho-Oregon border is actually deeper. But in his book, *The Snake River,* author Tim Palmer says that's wrong. "Sorry, Idahoans, but you still see this error all the time, propagated by regional, state, and private tourism promoters. Even the official Idaho highway map calls it the deepest canyon," *Idaho Statesman* reporter Dana Oland wrote in an article disputing the claim. Palmer says that Kings Canyon in California's Sierra Nevada Mountains is even deeper because Spanish Mountain is 8,240 feet above the Kings River, while Idaho's He Devil Mountain is 7,900 feet above the Snake River. By contrast the Grand Canyon of the Colorado is a mere 4,000 to 5,500 feet deep from rim to river.

Plenty of sources—including the federal Hells Canyon National Recreation Area website—still call Hells Canyon the deepest river gorge in North America. The Idaho state highway map lists He Devil with an elevation of 9,393 feet, and the Hells Canyon National Recreation Area website says that at its east rim the canyon is 8,043 feet above the river—but that's still shy of the 8,240 feet at Kings Canyon. Measured from He Devil Mountain, however, Hells Canyon would be deeper.

Whatever the statistics say, Hells Canyon is an awesome place. Visit or call the Hells Canyon National Recreation Area office at 1339 US 95 in Riggins for maps and detailed directions into the canyon. The phone number is (208) 628–3916, and the website is fs.fed.us/hellscanyon. (Also see the Southwestern Idaho chapter for information on trips from Hells Canyon Dam west of Cambridge.)

almost everything on the menu between $12 and $20. There's a full bar, or walk next door to ***Brodock's Saloon,*** where booths, tables, and even couches are grouped for easy conversation and where Albert Bierstadt prints and Thomas Moran artwork grace the walls.

The town of Harpster, east of Grangeville on Highway 13, serves as the gateway to another historic roadway off the beaten path. The ***Elk City Wagon Road*** was developed in the late nineteenth century as a route to the gold mines of central Idaho. Earlier still, the Nez Perce on their seasonal rounds used the trail as a way from the Camas Prairie to the Bitterroot Valley in Montana. The 53-mile, mostly unpaved road doesn't appear much different now than it did a hundred years ago. Today, however, drivers can expect to traverse it in four to six hours instead of days. Most passenger cars can travel this route if drivers take it slow, but large RVs or vehicles towing trailers aren't advised to make the trip.

Because snow and landslides restrict travel most of the year, the Elk City Road is generally only open late June through Sept. To find it, look for a sign describing the wagon road and turn right if you're coming from Grangeville (left if you've come from Kooskia to the north). Check in advance to be sure the road is open, make sure your vehicle is in good condition, and fuel up before you go—there are no filling stations along the way, although gas, food, and lodging are available in Elk City. The return trip from Elk City to Harpster via Highway 14, itself quite scenic, is 50 miles and takes about an hour and a half to drive. A self-guiding brochure to the road can be found online or at the US Forest Service offices in Kamiah, White Bird, or Elk City. For more information on road conditions, call the Red River Ranger District at (208) 842-2245.

Elk City also offers access to Dixie and **Red River Hot Springs.** Red River Hot Springs, about 25 miles off Highway 14, is a very rustic resort with rooms and cabins for overnight stays plus pools for swimming and soaking. Call (208) 842-2587 for reservations. There's some food service at the resort, but it's best to get groceries in Elk City before making the drive. Dixie, 32 miles south of Elk City—with all but the last 4 miles paved—caters to hunters, anglers, and snowmobile enthusiasts.

Elk City is the western gateway to an even more remote Idaho travel experience on the **Magruder Road,** a mostly unimproved 101-mile route created by the Civilian Conservation Corps in the 1930s. The road serves as the boundary between the Selway-Bitterroot Wilderness to the north and the Frank Church–River of No Return Wilderness to the south. Together, the two areas take in 3.5 million acres, twice the size of Delaware and Rhode Island combined.

You could drive the Magruder Road one-way to Darby, Montana, in one very long day, but most people take at least two days and make a camping trip of it. It's especially busy in the fall for hunting season, so casual travelers may prefer to visit in late July or August, though ATV riders are out in force then, too. High-clearance vehicles are recommended, and trailers are discouraged due to several hairpin turns along the way. There are no services along the route, so be sure to get food, fuel, and drinking water before you leave Elk City. Plan to practice leave-no-trace camping, whether you choose a spot in one of the designated primitive campgrounds or stake an unofficial site, which is permitted. For an informative brochure with maps, campsite information, and leave-no-trace camping tips, search online for Magruder Road Corridor or stop at the Elk City Ranger Station.

Back on US 95, the **White Bird Grade** south of Grangeville is one of Idaho's most notable highway achievements. Before it was completed in 1975, it took 13 hours to drive from Boise to Grangeville—a distance of 197 miles. The grade replaced a tortuous old road that took 14 miles to climb 2,900 feet. (An Idaho historical marker overlooking the old road notes that if all the old route's curves and switchbacks were placed together, they'd make thirty-seven complete circles.) Yet the old White Bird Road was itself an engineering marvel, built from 1915 to 1921 at a cost of $400,000 to replace a wagon road. The old route—the only road linking Northern Idaho to the state capital—was finally paved in 1938. In 1974, the year before its replacement opened, the grade was added to the National Register of Historic Places.

The old White Bird Road is easily seen east of the present highway, which takes just over 7 miles to climb 3,000 feet. Stop at the pullout for a sweeping view of White Bird Canyon. This was the site of the opening battle in the Nez Perce War, described earlier. As you'll recall, several young nontreaty Nez Perce seeking revenge for the death of one of their fathers and angered by their forced move to the reservation killed a number of white settlers. In response General Oliver Otis Howard dispatched ninety-nine men led by Captain David Perry to confront the Nez Perce at the Salmon River near here. Although they were poorly armed and outnumbered by the white men, the Nez Perce successfully turned back the Army while suffering no casualties of their own. From here the tribe started the three-and-a-half month, 1,000-mile retreat that finally ended with Chief Joseph's surrender in Montana.

White Bird Summit Lodge Bed & Breakfast perches in the high country just a mile from US 95. Rooms rent from about $120, including breakfast, swimming in an indoor pool, access to a barbecue area, and amazing views. Added adventure options include trail rides, Salmon River rafting, or Snake River jet boat trips. For more details or reservations, call (208) 983-1802 or see whitebirdsummitlodge.com.

The small towns of White Bird, Lucile, and Riggins serve as outfitting stops for the Salmon River as well as for treks into Hells Canyon National Recreation Area and the Hells Canyon Wilderness. ***Killgore Adventures*** in White Bird specializes in jet boat tours into the heart of Hells Canyon and guided fishing and hunting trips. The family-run business also offers RV camping and some indoor accommodations just off US 95. Call (800) 469-8757 or see killgore adventures.com for more information.

For an inspiring, top-down look at Hells Canyon, turn west off of US 95 onto Forest Road 517 for the 18-mile road to ***Heaven's Gate.*** This road, generally open from the Fourth of July until early Oct, can be managed by any passenger car (although trailers shouldn't make the climb). The first 8 miles are easily traversed; after that, the road gets washboarded, but the views make it all worthwhile. At Windy Saddle follow the signs for Heaven's Gate. A 350-yard trail climbs to a vista point at 8,429-feet elevation with dead-on views of the Seven Devils Range and the rest of the surrounding countryside. On a clear day you might see all the way into Montana. Unfortunately, the lookout at Heaven's Gate is only occasionally staffed by volunteers, and the interpretive signs could be better, but these are among the most memorable views in the Northwest.

US 95 in Riggins is lined with businesses catering to the traveler. The **Salmon Rapids Lodge,** sitting at the confluence of the Salmon and Little Salmon Rivers, is a cut above the average chain motel. A big indoor pool, outdoor spa, and a lovely two-story Great Room make this a restful stop. See photos at salmonrapids.com or call (877) 957-2743 for information. There are a half-dozen good restaurants and bars within walking distance.

You can't drive to the **Shepp Ranch** (located about 45 miles from Riggins), but they'll send a jet boat to pick you up. Once at Shepp Ranch, guests enjoy boating, rafting, trail riding, fishing, and hiking. Meals served family style feature the bounty of Idaho—trout, berries, vegetables from the ranch garden, and homemade bread, pies, and cakes. This is a place to truly get unplugged, because there's no cell phone service and no TV. Rates run about $325 per adult per day, including meals and activities. Family reunion alert: Groups of twelve or more people get the place to themselves. For more information call (208) 866-4268 or see sheppranch.com.

A spur off US 95 south of Riggins leads to Pollock, a small community along the Little Salmon River. The **Little Salmon Lodge** has a dozen guest rooms priced from $110 to $230 a night, a beer and wine bar, a riverside hot tub, and a friendly vibe. Call (800) 727-9977 or see details at littlesalmonlodge .com. The lodge is run in tandem with longtime outfitter **Northwest Voyageurs,** which offers custom multisport adventures in Idaho and beyond. For more information call (866) 669-0601 or see voyageurs.com.

US 95 continues along the Little Salmon to New Meadows. At that point, we've crossed over into what Idaho's tourism office calls Southwestern Idaho, but that's necessary to reach our final North Central Idaho destinations: the towns of Burgdorf and Warren.

At New Meadows turn onto Highway 55. Just before you reach Payette Lake and McCall, hang a left to head north on the Warren Wagon Road. The road is paved nearly to the Burgdorf turnoff (Forest Road 246, to the north), then it turns into gravel. Allow about an hour for travel to Warren, which sits about 44 miles from the highway. The route passes through a lot of timberland ravaged by forest fires in 1994, but signs of renewed forest growth can be seen, too.

Burgdorf Hot Springs, about 30 miles from McCall, is a popular soaking spot dating back to 1870. There are two pools—a large one, 5 feet deep, in which the temperature ranges from 98°F to 104°F, and a small children's wading pool—plus several hot tubs. Pool admission is $8 for adults, $5 for children. Rental bathing suits and towels are available if you forgot yours.

Sixteen cabins, most built between the 1870s and 1930s, sleep from two to twelve people. Rates (which include pool privileges) are $50 per adult single occupancy or $40 per adult double occupancy. Children in the same cabin cost $15 apiece. The cabins come equipped with woodstoves, beds, and outhouses, but guests need to bring their own bedding, cooking and lighting gear, and food. No tents or RVs are allowed, but there are several Forest Service campgrounds nearby, with one right next door. You can buy a few supplies including propane and snacks at Burgdorf, but it's wise to stock up ahead of time.

Although the road from McCall closes between Nov and mid-May, people come to Burgdorf all year long, usually by snowmobile, sometimes by cross-country skis. (There are 38 miles of groomed cross-country trails in the area.) Year-round this is an excellent spot to see wildlife: deer, elk, moose, and even the occasional black bear and mountain lion. For more information call (208) 636-3036 or visit burgdorfhotsprings.com.

Return to the Warren Wagon Road for the final 13 miles toward Warren. On the way the road passes through a community of private homes known as Secesh Meadows. Secesh is short for secessionist; seems there were quite a few Southern sympathizers among those mining here in the mid-nineteenth century. The **Secesh Stage Stop** sells gasoline, meals, and snacks to people passing through the area, and it has a few rooms and campsites available, too. Nearby, the Forest Service's Chinook Campground is a trailhead for the Secesh to Loon Lake Trail, part of the Idaho Centennial Trail. Aside from being a fairly easy trail, the path provides access to a fascinating and little-known artifact from Idaho history: the wreckage of a B-23 bomber. (See sidebar.)

Warren isn't literally the end of the road, but it's darn close. From here it's just a few bumpy miles to the edge of the Frank Church–River of No Return Wilderness, the largest in the lower forty-eight United States. About a dozen

In Plane View

Here's how a Payette National Forest brochure tells it: On January 29, 1943, flying from Nevada back to Tacoma, Washington, a B-23 bomber made an emergency landing on frozen Loon Lake near Warren. The "Dragon Bomber" slid across the ice and 150 feet into the nearby trees, both its wings sheared off. All eight men aboard survived, with a broken kneecap the only injury.

But the crew had no radio, and they were stranded. After waiting five days for rescue, they decided to send three men for help. The trio, carrying a shotgun and chocolate, hiked about 42 miles over two weeks through waist-deep snow before reaching the Lake Fork Guard Station. Once there, they were able to contact the Forest Service in McCall, which sent assistance. Today, hikers can still see the **B-23 Dragon Bomber wreckage** near the south side of the lake. For more information, photos, and directions, see the Dragon Bomber Crash site page at secesh.net.

people live year-round in Warren, maybe three times that number in summer. The town has no electricity, but it did get phone lines in 1995.

Warren may not have many people, but it has plenty of history. Established in 1862 with the discovery of gold, this is one of Idaho's oldest towns. In its first boom, Warren had 2,000 people. By 1870 many of these first miners had left, but more than a thousand Chinese miners had moved in to try their luck. (Chinese mining artifacts can be seen at the Forest Service's Warren Guard Station, where you can also get a walking tour booklet.) Warren had another population boom in the 1930s when dredging resumed. Although Warren was again threatened by a 1989 forest fire in the nearby Whangdoodle Creek drainage (and by yet another nearby fire in 2007), the town survived, and many of the standing buildings are more than one hundred years old.

Places to Stay in North Central Idaho

MOSCOW

Best Western University Inn
1516 Pullman Rd.
(800) 325-8765
uinnmoscow.com
Moderate

LaQuinta Inn
185 Warbonnet Dr.
(208) 882-5365
laquintamoscow.com
Moderate

Little Green Guesthouse
1020 South Adams St.
(208) 669-1654
littlegreenguesthouse.com
Moderate

Super 8 Moscow
175 Peterson Dr.
(208) 883-1503
super8.com
Moderate

ELK RIVER

Elk River Lodge
(208) 866-3299
elkriverlodge.net
Inexpensive–Moderate

OROFINO

Best Western Plus Lodge at River's Edge
615 Main St.
(208) 476-9999
bestwestern.com
Moderate–Expensive

Helgeson Hotel
125 Johnson Ave.
(800) 404-5729
helgesonhotel.com
Inexpensive–Moderate

Riverside Motel
10560 Highway 12
(208) 476-5711
theriversidemotel.com
Inexpensive

PIERCE

OutBack Adventures
Main Street
(208) 464-2171
outbackidaho.com
Inexpensive–Moderate

POWELL

Lochsa Lodge
(208) 942-3405
lochsalodge.com
Moderate

LOWELL

Three Rivers Resort
(208) 926-4430
idaho3rivers.com
Inexpensive–Moderate

SYRINGA

River Dance Lodge
(866) 769-8747
riverdancelodge.com
Moderate–Expensive

KOOSKIA

Reflections Inn
US 12 east of town
(888) 926-0855
reflectionsinn.com
Moderate

STITES

Idaho Sportsman Lodge
103 East St.
(208) 926-4766
idahosportsmanlodge.com
Moderate

KAMIAH

Clearwater 12 Motel
108 East Third St.
(US 12 at Cedar)
(208) 935-2671
clearwater12motel.com
Inexpensive–Moderate

Hearthstone Lodge
US 12, milepost 64
(208) 935-1492
hearthstonelodge.com
Moderate–Expensive

Lewis Clark Resort
4243 US 12
(208) 935-2556
lewisclarkresort.com
Inexpensive

LEWISTON

Comfort Inn
2128 Eighth Ave.
(208) 798-8090
choicehotels.com
Moderate

Inn America Lewiston
702 21st St.
(208) 746-4600
innamerica.com
Inexpensive–Moderate

Red Lion Hotel
US 12 and 21st Street
(208) 799-1000
redlion.com
Moderate–Expensive

ELK CITY

Prospector Lodge and Cabins
(208) 842-2597
Inexpensive

Red River Hot Springs
(208) 842-2589
redriverhs.wix.com/redriverhotsprings
Inexpensive–Moderate

COTTONWOOD

Dog Bark Park
(208) 962-3647
dogbarkparkinn.com
Moderate

Inn at St. Gertrude
465 Keuterville Rd.
(208) 451-4321
innatstgertrude.com
Moderate

GRANGEVILLE

Downtowner Inn
113 East North St.
(208) 983-1110
Inexpensive

Elkhorn Lodge
822 Southwest First St.
(208) 983-1500
Inexpensive

Gateway Inn
700 West Main St.
(877) 983-1463
idahogatewayinn.com
Inexpensive

WHITE BIRD

White Bird Summit Lodge Bed & Breakfast
2141 Old White Bird Hill Rd.
(208) 983-1802
whitebirdsummitlodge.com
Moderate

RIGGINS

Big Iron Motel
515 North Main St.
(208) 628-3005
bigironmotel.com
Inexpensive–Moderate

Riverview Motel
708 US 95
(208) 628-3041
riverviewmotel.com
Inexpensive–Moderate

Salmon Rapids Lodge
1010 South Main St.
(877) 957-2743
salmonrapids.com
Moderate–Expensive

POLLOCK

Little Salmon Lodge
121 Old Pollock Rd.
(800) 727-9977
littlesalmonlodge.com
Moderate–Expensive

WARREN

The Baum Shelter
(208) 636-4393
baumsheltertoo.com
Moderate

Places to Eat in
North Central Idaho

MOSCOW

Bloom
(breakfast and brunch)
403 South Main St.
(208) 882-4279
Moderate

The Breakfast Club
(breakfast)
501 South Main St.
(208) 882-6481
Inexpensive–Moderate

Lodgepole
(New American)
106 North Main St.
(208) 882-2268
Moderate–Expensive

Nectar
(fine dining and wine bar)
105 West Sixth St.
(208) 882-5194
Moderate–Expensive

Patty's Mexican Kitchen
450 West Sixth St.
(208) 883-3984
Inexpensive–Moderate

POWELL

Lochsa Lodge
(American)
(208) 942-3405
Inexpensive–Moderate

LOWELL

**Ryan's Wilderness Inn
Cafe**
(American)
US 12
(208) 926-4706
Inexpensive

KOOSKIA

Kooskia Cafe
(American)
6 North Main St.
(208) 926-4351
Inexpensive

KAMIAH

**Hearthstone Bakery &
Tea House**
(American)
502 Main St.
(208) 935-1912
Inexpensive

Sacajawea Cafe
(American)
4243 US 12
(208) 935-2233
Inexpensive–Moderate

OROFINO

Dining on the Edge
(New American)
625 Main St.
(208) 476-7805
Moderate–Expensive

Ponderosa Restaurant
(American)
220 Michigan Ave.
(208) 476-4818
Inexpensive–Moderate

ALSO WORTH SEEING IN NORTH CENTRAL IDAHO

McConnell Mansion
Moscow

Dworshak National Fish Hatchery
Orofino

Clearwater River Casino
Lewiston

Camas Prairie Winery
Bovill

The Filling Station
(coffeehouse) Troy

LEWISTON

Bait Shop Grill
(breakfast and brunch)
3206 Fifth St.
(208) 746-1562
Inexpensive

Bojack's Broiler Pit
(steaks)
311 Main St.
(208) 746-9532
Moderate–Expensive

Hells Canyon Smokehouse
(barbecue)
145 Thain Rd.
(208) 816-1709
Moderate

Meriwether's Bistro
(American)
in the Red Lion Hotel
(208) 748-1151
Moderate–Expensive

Mystic Cafe
(breakfast, brunch, coffee)
1303 Main St.
(208) 743-1811
Inexpensive–Moderate

Thai Taste
1410 21st St.
(208) 746-6192
Inexpensive–Moderate

Waffles 'N' More
(American)
1421 Main St.
(208) 743-5189
Inexpensive

COTTONWOOD

Country Haus
(American)
407 Foster St.
(208) 962-3391
Inexpensive–Moderate

GRANGEVILLE

Oscar's Restaurant
(American)
101 East Main St.
(208) 983-2106
Moderate

Seasons Restaurant
(American)
124 West Main St.
(208) 983-4203
Inexpensive–Moderate

RIGGINS

Back Eddy Grill
(American)
533 North Main St.
(208) 628-9233
Inexpensive

Cattlemen's Family Dining
(American)
601 South Main St.
(208) 628-3195
Inexpensive

River Rock Cafe
(American)
1149 South Main St.
(208) 628-3434
Inexpensive

WARREN

The Baum Shelter
(American)
(208) 636-4393
Moderate

Southwestern Idaho

Southwestern Idaho is the Gem State's most varied region. It includes the fast-growing Boise metropolitan area of more than 675,000 people, yet it also contains several sprawling counties with fewer than 12,000 inhabitants. It is home to thriving health care and high-tech industries, but it also has a few towns that didn't receive telephone service until the mid-1990s.

Between the urban attractions and the neighboring back-country, there is no one best way to explore Southwestern Idaho, and it could easily take a week or more to cover the region. But here's my recommendation, the one you'll see used in this chapter:

Start on the shores of Payette Lake near McCall, the region's most popular resort area. From McCall, trek north to New Meadows, then southwest on US 95 to Cambridge, gateway to the Hells Canyon Scenic Byway and the upper reaches of Idaho's deepest gorge. After backtracking to Cambridge and New Meadows, you might want to head east from McCall into the wilderness areas near Yellow Pine and Warm Lake (and Burgdorf and Warren, covered in the North Central Idaho chapters but most accessible from McCall).

After returning to Highway 55, we'll travel the Payette River Scenic Byway, then veer off onto the back roads once again to survey the Boise Basin, rich in mining history. Then we'll visit the capital city of Boise, the Treasure Valley of suburbs and fast-disappearing farmland west of Boise, and the high desert outback of Owyhee and Elmore Counties.

For more Southwestern Idaho travel information, call the Southwest Idaho Travel Association at (800) 635-5240 or see visitsouthwestidaho.org.

Wilderness Gateways

McCall is one of Idaho's best vacation destinations, with a regionally noted ski area and a spacious lake at hand. No matter what season you visit McCall, you're bound to have a good time outdoors. Late spring through early fall, boats and watercraft of all kinds flit across the sparkling surface of Payette Lake. Plenty of snow each winter means abundant mountain recreation, whether you want to ski, snowboard, sled, or skate. And while outdoor fun is central here, McCall also offers good food, drink, and shopping.

Ponderosa State Park—one of the state's most popular—is a favorite for camping, hiking, biking, and boating in the warm months and cross-country skiing once the snow falls. Occupying a thousand-acre peninsula just across Payette Lake from McCall, Ponderosa is named for the tall pine trees that hug the lakeshore and cover the nearby mountainsides. It's just as rich in wildlife and wildflowers. For camping and recreation information, call (208) 634-2164 or see parksandrecreation.idaho.gov/parks/ponderosa.

For one of Idaho's most sublime paddling experiences, try canoeing or kayaking the gentle North Fork Payette River, accessed via the North Beach area, a separate unit of Ponderosa State Park entered along the Warren Wagon Road. (Take the turnoff from Highway 55 across from Lardo Grill & Saloon. The river put-in is about 6.5 miles from here.) *Backwoods Adventures* rents canoes, kayaks, and paddleboards at North Beach by the hour ($12 to $15) or half day (four hours; $36 to $45) during the summer months. Call (208) 469-9067 for reservations or see backwoodsadventuresmccall.com for more information.

Brundage Mountain—located 8 miles northwest of McCall via Highway 55—continues to attract a loyal following for its affordable prices and good variety of ski terrain. Full-day lift tickets run about $62 for adults and $23 to $37 for children and seniors, with discounts after 12:30 p.m. One of the lifts offers scenic rides in summer, too. Call (208) 634-7669 for the ski report, or see brundage.com for more information.

If Brundage is still too big for your tastes, or you're looking for a place to pinch a few extra pennies, the Payette Lakes Ski Club's *Little Ski Hill* will fill the bill nicely. T-bar lift tickets here cost a mere $15 for adults and $12 for children. It's located 2 miles north of McCall on Highway 55. Call (208) 634-5691 or see littleskihill.org for more information, including the hours, which generally run late afternoon until 9 or 10 p.m. Tues through Sat, late Dec through mid-Mar.

The biggest winter event in Southwestern Idaho—possibly the entire state—is the *McCall Winter Carnival.* Each year the festival draws about 100,000 people. A snow-sculpting competition is the big attraction, and there are also fireworks, a full-moon cross-country ski tour, dogsled races, wine tasting, and more. Winter Carnival takes place in late Jan or early Feb each year. For information phone the McCall Chamber of Commerce at (208) 634-7631. It's winter all year at the *Manchester Ice & Event Centre* at 200 East Lake St., where people skate year-round. See the hours at manchestericecenter.com.

McCall has one of the state's highest concentrations of vacation rentals, because many Boise-area families have cottages here that they use only a few times each year. *Johnson & Company Vacation Rentals* has a great roster of McCall-area accommodations for a longer stay. Call (208) 634-7134 or see idahoresortproperties.com for listings and last-minute deals. *InIdaho* is another highly useful tool for planning a McCall getaway. Travel counselors with this free service have up-to-date information and expertise to help you match activities and accommodations with your budget and tastes. Visit inidaho.com or call (800) 844-3246, and they'll help you out. And, of course, nationally known home-sharing sites including Airbnb, VRBO, and Vacasa all have McCall-area listings, too.

For those who seek a more traditional lodging experience, the venerable *Hotel McCall* has an excellent downtown location overlooking Payette Lake. Opened in 1904, the inn has modern rooms and many hospitable touches, including free DVD rentals, fresh flowers, warm homemade cookies each evening, and a continental breakfast each morning. Guests also have access to a well-stocked library and an indoor pool. High-season rates range from $150 for a room with two queen beds and a jetted tub to $300 for a condo that can sleep a family of four. For more information or reservations, call (866) 800-1183 or see hotelmccall.com.

Hotel McCall guests don't have to go far for a good meal. *Rupert's,* the hotel restaurant, features fine Northwest cuisine and a patio with a view of the lake. It's open for lunch and dinner. Call (208) 634-8108 for reservations. A courtyard behind the hotel features several shops selling all the makings for an instant picnic on the nearby lakeshore or at Ponderosa State Park.

Among McCall's other restaurants, the *Mill Supper Club* is one of the oldest and most interesting spots in town. The menu includes steak, prime rib, and seafood, and the decor features lots of antiques and what may be the

AUTHOR'S FAVORITES IN SOUTHWESTERN IDAHO

Hells Canyon Scenic Byway
West of Cambridge

Kayaking the North Fork of the Payette River
McCall

Boise River Greenbelt
Boise

Bruneau Dunes State Park
near Hammett

Idaho Anne Frank Human Rights Memorial
Boise

largest collection of beer taps anywhere in the United States—thousands of 'em displayed all over the restaurant and adjacent bar. Dinner is served seven nights a week starting at 5:30 p.m. The restaurant is at 324 North Third St. (Highway 55). Call (208) 634-7683 for reservations.

For breakfast or lunch, the **FoggLifter Cafe** is a good choice at 1003 North Third St. Named for backcountry pilot Bob Fogg, who also served as a mayor of McCall and member of the Idaho Legislature, the FoggLifter has fare priced from $3 (for a bagel and cream cheese) to about $8 for sandwiches. The rambling, pumpkin-colored interior is cozy in the cooler months, while lots of outdoor seating beckons when the weather is fine.

About 16 miles northwest of McCall, Highway 55 ends at US 95 in New Meadows. Turn south on US 95 to reach Cambridge, best known as the jumping-off spot for the **Hells Canyon Scenic Byway.** Although there are a few other ways to access Hells Canyon by vehicle, the byway is the only one

TOP ANNUAL EVENTS IN SOUTHWESTERN IDAHO

McCall Winter Carnival
(late Jan–early Feb)

Treefort
Boise (late Mar)

National Oldtime Fiddlers Championship
Weiser (third week of June)

Idaho Shakespeare Festival
Boise (June–Sept)

Yellow Pine Harmonica Fest
(first full weekend of Aug)

Western Idaho Fair
Garden City (late Aug)

Spirit of Boise Balloon Classic
Boise (late summer)

Art in the Park
Boise (early Sept)

usually open year-round. From Cambridge, Highway 71 crosses into Oregon at Brownlee Dam and back into the Gem State at Oxbow Dam. From Oxbow Dam, the Hells Canyon Scenic Byway—an Idaho Power–owned road open to the public—runs north to its terminus (and back into Oregon) at Hells Canyon Dam. There's some fine camping along the reservoirs behind these dams. Sites are first come, first served. Call (800) 422-3143 or visit idahopower.com/ourenvironment for information.

Many boat trips launch from below Hells Canyon Dam. Choose from either a rafting expedition of three to six days or, if your time and pocketbook are pressed, a jet-boat ride. For a complete list of outfitters traveling in Hells Canyon, see fs.fed.us/hellscanyon and search for Snake River trips. Jet-boat trips ranging from two hours to two days are run by **Hells Canyon Adventures,** which also does whitewater rafting/jet-boat combo trips. The company's two-hour trips are just long enough to give riders a taste of the canyon's scenery and history; they're also good choices for families with young children who aren't yet ready to brave big white water on the rafts. (HCA is fond of saying even babies and grandmas enjoy these trips.) Highlights include an up-close, bottom-up view of Hells Canyon Dam; a stop at an area known for its Native American pictographs; and an interpretation of early homestead life in Hells Canyon. A few of the stories you may hear verge on tall-tale territory, but all in all, this is an enjoyable and scenic trip.

The morning trip, which includes a riverside picnic lunch, starts at 10 a.m. Pacific time and costs $75 per person ages 12 and up and $38 for children ages 3 to 11. The afternoon trip begins at 2 p.m. with a cost of $60 per person age 12 or older and $35 per child ages 3 to 11. Allow about two and a half hours for the winding, 64-mile drive from Cambridge to Hells Canyon Dam. For more information on these tours or other Hells Canyon Adventures, call (800) 422-3568 or see hellscanyonadventures.com.

Aside from its role as Hells Canyon base camp, Cambridge is an interesting little town in its own right, as well as a major access point for the 85-mile Weiser River Trail (see sidebar). Check out the **Cambridge Museum** at the junction of US 95 and Highway 71 for fascinating exhibits such as one detailing the journey of Edith Clegg, who went upriver through Hells Canyon in 1939. The museum is open from Hells Canyon Days (held the first week in June) through Labor Day weekend from 11 a.m. to 4 p.m. Wed through Sat, or you can call (208) 257-3541 or 257-3485 for an appointment. **The Cambridge House,** built in 1916 at 95 South First St., offers modern bed-and-breakfast accommodations for about $110 a night. See thecambridgehouse.net for details and call (208) 257-3555 for reservations.

Weiser River Trail

Although North Idaho's Route of the Hiawatha and Trail of the Coeur d'Alenes get a lot of attention, the **Weiser River Trail** is now the longest nonmotorized multiple-use trail in Idaho. The 85-mile path runs along its namesake river and an abandoned railroad bed that was used by trains from about 1895 to 1995. Development of the trail began soon after, and the path received National Recreation Trail status in 2010.

The trail is still a work in progress, and very much a labor of love for the Friends of the Weiser River Trail, a volunteer organization that is developing the pathway from Weiser to near New Meadows a bit at a time. There are some easy paved sections near Weiser, Cambridge, and Council (all of which also have places to stay); the rest ranges from graded rail-bed ballast material to gravel and dirt.

The Cambridge–Midvale stretch of the trail, near its midway point, is a good overnight destination from either end of the route. **Mundo Hot Springs,** 3 miles north of Cambridge, has a campground and hostel accommodations for up to seven people in a single room (for $80), plus a natural mineral water pool and bistro open to the public. See mundohotsprings.com or call (208) 257-3849. Comfy accommodations— including one private room with a queen-size bed for $60, a family room to sleep six for $100, or dorm bunks for $25—also are available at **Trailhead Guesthouse and Hostel,** just a half a mile from the trail in Midvale (which is 31 miles from the Weiser trailhead and 8 miles south of Cambridge). The hostel also offers a shared common room, well-equipped kitchen, Wi-Fi, secure storage, and a fenced area for horses. Groups of up to eighteen people can rent the whole house for $285 a night. Call (208) 473-6292 or see trailheadhostel.com for reservations.

Several sections of the Weiser River Trail parallel US 95, making it easy to pull over and pedal or walk a while on a short out-and-back adventure. For the latest news and amenities popping up along the trail (including camping, pet accommodations, and shuttle services), plus special events including a wagon train and organized bike rides, see weiserrivertrail.org.

Two other scenic day trips out of the McCall area lead to some of Idaho's most cherished yet accessible backcountry destinations. North of McCall, the Warren Wagon Road leads to Burgdorf Hot Springs and the former mining town of Warren. (See the end of the North Central Idaho chapter for details on this route.) Another route leading east from McCall travels to Yellow Pine and Warm Lake before looping back to Highway 55 at Cascade. The road from McCall to Yellow Pine, Forest Road 48, is a rough but scenic route passable by any vehicle in good condition driven by a motorist using care. The road runs alongside boulder fields and immense rock outcroppings, along with areas where extensive wildfire damage is visible; this region is among those most heavily damaged by forest fires in recent years.

A few spots along the way are worth noting. The ***Duck Lake Trail,*** just a mile long, is among the easier high-country paths you'll find in these rugged parts. It's not far east of Lick Creek Summit, and the trailhead is well signed. And near the junction of Road 48 and the Salmon River Road (Forest Road 674), there's an exhibit that explains the history of the Chinese miners who toiled in the area a century ago. From 1870 through 1900, in fact, the Chinese miners had a three-to-one majority among prospectors working the Warren mining district.

Yellow Pine, with a year-round population of about fifty, is surprisingly bustling despite its remote location. Yellow Pine folks also have a nifty sense of humor: Witness the University of Yellow Pine sign on the town's one-room schoolhouse. Most Idaho towns have an annual community bash or two, and Yellow Pine is no exception. The ***Yellow Pine Harmonica Fest,*** held the first full weekend of August, typically attracts thirty contestants and about 1,200 spectators who crowd the tiny town for the mouth harp competition and other musical events, as well as barbecues, breakfasts, community potlucks, and a street fair. If you want to attend the festival, odds are you'll be camping out, though the ***Yellow Pine Lodge*** has a dozen rooms and the general store has a few, too. The Yellow Pine, Idaho, Facebook page is the best online source for updated local info.

Nine miles south of Yellow Pine on Forest Road 413, ***Wapiti Meadow Ranch*** offers access to excellent fly-fishing, plus hiking, mountain biking, panning for gold, and exploring nearby ghost towns. Wapiti Meadow is no misnomer: Guests really are likely to see elk, especially in springtime, along with deer, moose, coyotes, and maybe a black bear or gray wolf. Four cabins are outfitted with living rooms and sleeping quarters as well as fully equipped kitchens. Rates start at $100 per night and $600 for a week, and fishing rods, reels, and waders can be reserved in advance, too. For more information or reservations, call (208) 633-3217 or see wapitimeadowranch.com.

Forest Road 413 continues south from Wapiti Meadow to Landmark, site of a Boise National Forest ranger station. From there a good paved road takes a steep and winding plunge through heavily timbered country to Warm Lake, a resort and vacation home area. In summertime, fishing and hiking are big draws, while hunters throng here in the fall and snowmobilers and cross-country skiers arrive in winter. ***North Shore Lodge*** has ten cabins, some with cooking facilities, priced from $85 to $160 a night. The on-site restaurant serves breakfast, lunch, and dinner. Call (208) 632-2000 or see northshorelodgeidaho .com for more information. There's also camping nearby.

The Warm Lake Road ends up back in Cascade, at the south end of a long, broad valley with expansive views that are a contrast to the tight river canyons to the south. Together with Donnelly, its neighboring town 16 miles to the north, Cascade is a major recreation hub. The area was the site of Idaho's first twenty-first-century land rush with the development of **Tamarack Resort** on the west shores of Lake Cascade. Tamarack's first phase opened in 2004, and it was eventually supposed to be the largest destination resort built in North America in a quarter-century. But the development was verging on bankruptcy even before the recession hit later that decade, and there has been plenty of legal wrangling over its future ever since. Still, some pretty sweet amenities remain, including lift-serviced mountain-biking terrain, zip-line tours, hiking trails, watercraft rentals, and plenty of lodging options. For the latest updates, see tamarackidaho.com.

Just 1 mile east of Donnelly off of Highway 55, the historic community of **Roseberry** is home to some cool events including a mid-July music festival and Wednesday night concert series in July and August. **Gold Fork Hot Springs** is another special spot far enough from the highway to deter crowds, with pools in a lovely rock-rimmed setting. Admission is $8 for adults and $6 for children age 11 and younger. It opens at noon daily except Tues, when it's closed. Watch for the blue-and-white signs pointing the way from Highway 55, and call (208) 890-8730 or see goldforkhotsprings.com for more information.

With nearly 50 square miles of surface and 86 miles of shoreline, there's room to spread out on Lake Cascade, the region's largest. **Lake Cascade State Park** is a favorite for boating (of course), camping, and windsurfing. The park has a half-dozen units arrayed along the lake's west shore (accessible via Donnelly) and another nine areas along the east shore, mostly near Cascade. Also close to town and part of the park, the **Crown Point Trail** on an old railroad bed gets year-round use by snow enthusiasts in winter and hikers and cyclists the rest of the year. See parksandrecreation.idaho.gov/parks/lake cascade for maps and more information.

The town of Cascade is mostly a pit stop for people heading to and from the rivers, lakes, and parks nearby, but it has done a good job developing its own in-town diversions including **Kelly's Whitewater Park** on the North Fork of the Payette River, which hosts both national kayaking competitions and paddle-sports camps for local children. See kellyswhitewaterpark.com for details and coming events. Nearby at 762 South Main St., **River Gear** sells and rents river toys and accessories, and it's a good spot for advice on running any of the region's rivers. Call (208) 382-6580 or see rivergearcascade.com. **The Strand** riverside trail links the Water's Edge RV Park at Cascade's north edge with the whitewater park and Fischer Pond Park near the south end of town.

South of Cascade, the Payette River can't help but command the traveler's attention, with plenty of handy pullouts for fishing, picnicking, or even taking a dip on a scorching summer day. Keep the camera handy, too: The graceful yet sturdy Rainbow Bridge south of Cascade is one of Idaho's most picturesque. If you'd like to get out on the river, **Cascade Raft and Kayak** offers guided whitewater floats that range from mild to wild. Half-day trips start at $45 for adults and $30 for kids. For more info or reservations, call (800) 292-7238 or see cascaderaft.com. Hang a left at Banks for a trip into the Boise Basin, a former mining hotbed still rich in scenic wealth. (Note: Don't confuse the Boise Basin with the Boise metro area. To get to Boise—the city—from Banks, keep driving south on Highway 55 and hang a left at the town of Eagle.)

The Boise Basin

The two-lane Banks-Lowman Highway, also known as the Wildlife Canyon Scenic Byway, wasn't paved until the 1990s. Most of it runs along the South Fork of the Payette River, and it also offers access to the popular Garden Valley vacation home area.

Eight miles east of Banks, turn left off the highway to travel a mile to the hamlet of Crouch. You'll find several down-home restaurants and shops here, along with the **Starlight Mountain Theatre,** which presents Broadway musicals outdoors each summer. Tickets run $10 to $25, with dinner available for an extra fee Thurs through Sat with 24 hours' notice. For more information call (208) 462-5523 or see starlightmt.com. Four miles north of Crouch, Terrace Lakes Resort features a challenging golf course, a geothermal pool, a restaurant, and overnight lodging priced from $60 to $175. Call (208) 462-3250 or see terracelakes.com. **Idaho Cabin Keepers** offers several dozen fully furnished cabins and vacation homes in the Garden Valley area, priced from about $100 a night, with a two-night minimum. Browse the offerings online at idahovaca tioncabins.com or call (877) 322-2467 for personalized help.

At Lowman, Highway 21 treks north to Stanley and south to Idaho City. A short spur off the northern stretch leads to Grandjean. This tiny town on the western slope of the Sawtooth Mountains is just outside the Sawtooth Wilderness Area boundaries. Grandjean was named for the Boise National Forest's "grandfather," Emile Grandjean, first supervisor of the forest from 1908 to 1919.

Grandjean is home to the **Sawtooth Lodge.** More accurately you could say the Sawtooth Lodge is Grandjean. The lodge serves continental breakfast and lunch daily plus dinner on Friday and Saturday, with hearty mountain fare and huckleberry shakes topping the bill. No-frills log cabins, most heated by wood stoves, sleep from two to four people at prices ranging from about $85 to $125 a night. (The least-expensive cabins share bathroom facilities. There are also outdoor grills plus pots and pans for guests who need them.) Guests have access to a warm mineral-water plunge pool, wildlife viewing, hiking, and fishing. RV and tent-camping facilities are available, too, and it also should be noted that Grandjean makes an ideal vacation destination for folks with disabilities; one of the Sawtooth Lodge's cabins is outfitted for people with disabilities, and a mile-long nature trail is wheelchair accessible.

Sawtooth Lodge usually opens Memorial Day and closes after Labor Day. For current rates, reservations, or other information, call (208) 259-3331 or see sawtoothlodge.com.

Although not as well known as the forty-niners' rush to the California gold fields or the boom in the Yukon, Idaho miners had glory days all their own. During the 1860s more gold was mined from the mountains northeast of Boise than from all of Alaska. In fact, Idaho City was once the largest city in the Northwest, and like most mining towns, it had a reputation as a wild place. It's been reported that only 28 of the 200 people buried in the town's Boot Hill died a natural death. These days, however, it's much more calm—even peaceful—with a small selection of visitor services and abundant recreation nearby. The areas around Idaho City are justly famous for great hiking and cross-country skiing.

Stop by the town visitor center at the corner of Highway 21 and Main Street for a leaflet describing notable Idaho City buildings. Among them, the old 1867 post office at 503 Montgomery St. now serves as the **Boise Basin Museum,** open Mon through Sat from 11 a.m. to 4 p.m. and Sun from 1 to 4 p.m. Memorial Day through Labor Day and sometimes in Sept if the weather cooperates. Guided walking tours of Idaho City are sometimes possible if you call ahead and make arrangements; call (208) 392-4550 for information.

For a meal in Idaho City, try **Trudy's Kitchen** at 419 Highway 21. This locally popular restaurant serves hearty breakfasts, bodacious hamburgers, and a house salad drizzled with huckleberry vinaigrette dressing. Sandwiches range in price from about $7 to $11, with dinner entrees priced from about $11 to $18. Trudy's is open daily at 8 a.m. and closes at about 8 p.m. (9 p.m. on Fri and Sat). The phone number is (208) 392-4151.

The area around Idaho City is known for some of the best cross-country skiing in the state: Eighteen miles north of town on Highway 21, the Whoop-Um-Up Park N' Ski area has 6.6 miles of marked trails, with sections suitable for all skier levels. Another 2 miles north, Gold Fork Park N' Ski accesses 21.4 miles of groomed trails, with terrain best for advanced beginners to serious skiers. Banner Ridge Park N' Ski, 3.5 miles from Gold Fork, has 22 miles of groomed trails for intermediate and expert skiers, plus off-trail bowl skiing. Gold Fork and Banner Ridge both have yurts available for rent. For more information call the Idaho Department of Parks and Recreation at (208) 334-4199 or see parks andrecreation.idaho.gov/activities/yurts.

Another side trip off of Highway 21 leads to **Atlanta,** a late bloomer among Idaho's mining districts and a scenic little town well worth the long drive, as long as you are self-sufficient because there are few visitor services. On one hand, several roads in the Boise Basin head toward Atlanta. On the other hand, none of them is easy—and some (notably Forest Road 126, the way from Rocky Bar) are sort of scary. The most popular routes are the heavily rutted—68-mile Middle Fork Road (Forest Road 268) from Lucky Peak Reservoir near Boise and the 40-mile combination of the Edna Creek (384), North Fork Boise River (327), and Middle Fork Boise Roads. Check with the Forest Service office in Idaho City at (208) 392-6681 for information on road conditions. Logging trucks often work these highways, so be an attentive, cautious driver. Be sure to have a full tank of gas before you head out for Atlanta since no fuel is available.

Atlanta doesn't have tourist attractions, but that's the point: People come here to relax and escape the pace and clutter of modern life. There's a Forest Service cabin for rent (unless fire crews are using it)—search for Atlanta cabin at recreation.gov—and the **Beaver Lodge** has rooms for rent and a cafe. See beaverlodgeatlanta.com or call (208) 864-2132. Two nearby hot springs beckon bathers, too. To find **Atlanta Hot Springs,** drive a mile east of town and look for the little parking area on the right-hand side of the road just past the big green pond. (No, the pond is not the hot spring!) The choice spot, **Chattanooga Hot Springs,** is much nicer, sitting below a waterfall in a rock pool on the Middle Fork of the Boise River. But it's also a bit harder to find. To get there, look for the spur road just west of Atlanta Hot Springs (but on the other side of the road) and follow it about 0.3 mile north. The road ends at the top of a bluff. Cross a small stream and hike down the bluff to the hot springs. The road leading to the bluff is marked private property, but hot springs enthusiasts say that if you stay on the road and refrain from rowdiness, you're OK.

From Atlanta, you can either backtrack along the Forest Service roads to Highway 21 or take the rugged southern routes (Forest Service Roads 126 or 156) to Rocky Bar and the Featherville-Pine-Trinity Lakes area. (See the "Snake River Vistas" section later in this chapter for more information on this region.)

Highway 21 intersects with Interstate 84 on the eastern edge of Boise. Before starting your urban explorations, however, you might want to head east for a few miles to get your first look at Idaho's capital city as its forebears did, from **Bonneville Point.** This was the spot from which mountain men and Oregon Trail pioneers first spied the verdant Boise River Valley below. Boise got its name, in fact, when a party of French trappers visited Bonneville Point in 1833. For weeks the trappers had seen nothing but lava and sagebrush. Now, far below but after less than a day's walk, they saw a verdant river valley, the stream bank lined with trees. "*Les bois, les bois, voyez les bois*" ("The trees, the

Leave Your Watch at Home

Time really does slow down in Atlanta, and it sometimes comes to a complete stop. Upon my arrival at the Forest Service rental cabin, I was surprised to see a clock on the kitchen wall. I soon realized it wasn't working, however, and I felt better. Who needs a clock in Atlanta?

Alas, my sleep was restless that night. The first time I awoke, I pulled on my pants and shoes and went outside to survey the stars. With no earthbound lights to compete, the heavens were magnificent, even by jaded Idaho standards. The Milky Way stood out like a gossamer scarf flung across the sky, and the Pleiades glittered like a diamond bracelet. I did not look at my watch, but I knew it was well after midnight.

The next time I stirred, it seemed to be dawn. I reached for my watch on the bedside table, surprised to see it was only 2:40 a.m. How could this be, I wondered? Before long I understood that my watch, like the kitchen clock, had stopped. Perhaps that is the message of Idaho's remote places: Leave your watch—and anything else that tells time—tucked out of sight. Time doesn't matter out here, and you can learn all you need to know by the angle of the sun, the still of the night, and the sound of your own heartbeat.

trees, look at the trees"), the trappers supposedly cried in joy. To this day Boise is known as the "City of Trees."

To find Bonneville Point, take exit 64 off I-84 and follow the signs north. The Bureau of Land Management has placed an interpretive kiosk at the site, and a long stretch of wagon-wheel ruts may be seen nearby, along with a good look at Boise and its foothills. "When we arrived at the top we got a grand view of the Boise River Valley," emigrant Cecilia E. M. Adams noted in her diary. The trees they saw, she added, were "the first we have seen in more than a month." Likewise, explorer John Frémont, who mapped the West, wrote of his joy in seeing the Boise River, "a beautiful rapid stream, with clear mountain water" and noted he was "delighted this afternoon to make a pleasant camp under fine old trees again."

City of Trees

With a population of about 218,000, Boise rivals Spokane and Tacoma to be the third-largest city in the Northwest, after the much-bigger Seattle and Portland. But with a metro area of well over a half-million people, Boise and its suburbs definitely have been discovered by young professionals who want to cap off a day of work with a microbrew or a mountain bike ride; by families seeking a city environment that still feels "small town"; and by retirees who like the lively but livable pace.

Boise may be growing, but its downtown remains wonderfully compact, with many of its most interesting sites within walking distance. Looming over all is the **State Capitol** at 700 West Jefferson St., and although Idaho's most famous building isn't "off the beaten path," its interior harbors some little-known and fascinating lore. For example, a replica of the *Winged Victory of Samothrace* stands here. The original, sculpted around 300 BC, is in the Louvre in Paris; in 1949 France gave a replica to each American state as a gesture of thanks following World War II, but Idaho's copy is supposedly the only one on public view in a statehouse. Then there's the one-of-a-kind statue of George Washington astride a horse. The statue was created by Charles Ostner, a self-trained artist, Austrian immigrant, and Payette River ferry operator who worked for four years by candlelight to carve the statue from a single piece of yellow pine. No one is sure what the statue is worth, but the Smithsonian Institution reportedly once sought—unsuccessfully—to add the work to its collections. Ostner presented the bronzed statue to the Idaho territorial government in 1869. It stood outside on the capitol grounds for decades but was eventually brought indoors, restored, and covered with gold leaf.

When the Idaho Legislature is in session (generally January through early spring), the Capitol is open from 6 a.m. to 10 p.m. Mon through Fri. The rest of the year, it's open from 6 a.m. to 6 p.m. Mon through Fri. Weekend hours year-round are 9 a.m. to 5 p.m. Pick up a self-guided tour booklet at the Capitol or access it online at legislature.idaho.gov.

A few blocks east of the Capitol, the **Boise Guest House** at 614 North Fifth St. is a convenient place to stay within walking distance of downtown. Its six suites priced from about $100 to $200 a night each have kitchen facilities and private bathrooms, plus bicycles for rent and baby gear to borrow if you're traveling with a tot. (Pets are welcome in several of the suites, too.) Boise Guest House has more accommodations available in the nearby North End neighborhood; see details on its website at boiseguesthouse.com.

The area southeast of the statehouse, known as Old Boise, is one of the city's busiest nightlife districts, and it has an array of restaurants and stores, too. **Flying M,** at 500 West Idaho St., is a popular coffeehouse with strong local flavor and a quirky gift shop. (Flying M has a "coffee garage" in Nampa, too, at 1314 Second St. South.) One block south, **Pengilly's Saloon** at 513 Main St. has been written up everywhere from *Esquire* to *Cosmopolitan.* Adult-friendly acoustic, blues, and jazz music make this a great place to enjoy a drink and soak in a little history. Call (208) 345-6344 or check its Facebook page to find out who's playing.

The corner of Sixth and Main is party central for downtown Boise, but it also has two good restaurant choices that share an entrance at 105 South Sixth

Eating and Drinking in Boise

Many Boise visitors are surprised at the wealth of dining and drinking options in this small city, but they shouldn't be: Although it's hundreds of miles inland, Boise benefits from its relative proximity to the Pacific Northwest, one of the world's great regions for eating and dining. West Coast food trends don't take long to arrive here, but the city revels in tried-and-true fare, too, from great breakfast joints, locally owned lunch counters, neighborhood pizzerias, and enticing ethnic eateries that range from simple to high concept.

Your best sources of current information on area restaurants include *Boise Weekly* (the local alternative newspaper) and the *Idaho Statesman*'s weekly *Scene* magazine. Both are widely available for free in newsstand boxes around town, as well as online at boiseweekly.com and idahostatesman.com, and are also good resources for local arts and entertainment offerings.

Finally, special shout-outs to two Boise restaurants where you can eat for a good cause. *Life's Kitchen* is a longtime Boise nonprofit that trains young adults who've had rough lives for careers in the restaurant business. Its cafe serves lunch from 11 a.m. to 1 p.m. Tues through Fri at 1025 South Capitol Blvd. Learn more and check the weekly menu at lifeskitchen.org. *Even Stevens Sandwiches* at 815 West Bannock St. tallies up all the sandwiches it sells every month and donates enough ingredients for nonprofit partners to make that many sandwiches for hungry people. It's open daily and sells salads, breakfast, and brunchy stuff, too.

St. *Reef* (upstairs) is an island-themed bar and restaurant that often has live music, while the *Front Door* specializes in inspired beer and pizza pairings. On the northeast corner of the intersection, have a look around the historic *Pioneer Tent Building.* Among other shops and restaurants, the independent crafters of *Idaho Made* have a cooperative shop here. Stop in to peruse their selection of creative handmade treasures.

Anchoring the corner of Main Street and North Capitol, the *Egyptian Theatre* opened in 1927 and nearly closed for good until local preservationists restored its gilded glory in 1999. It hosts concerts and is also the venue for a classic film series with screenings suggested by local movie buffs. See egyptian theatre.net and boiseclassicmovies.com for upcoming shows. *The Flicks* at 646 Fulton St. on the south edge of downtown is another draw for Boise cinema lovers, serving light cafe fare and screening independent and foreign films. Both venues are an easy walk from one of downtown's newest hotels, the *Inn at 500 Capitol,* with balconies, fireplaces, loaner bicycles, and room service discreetly delivered via a butler pantry between the hallway and the room.

West of Capitol Boulevard, the *Capital City Public Market* is held along Eighth Street each Sat morning from mid-Apr through mid-Dec. Vendors from all over Southwestern Idaho line the sidewalks to sell fresh food, plants, arts and crafts, and more. (While you're in the neighborhood, duck into *Rediscovered Books* at 180 North Eighth St., an indie bookstore that's a thriving spot for author events and finding something wonderful to read.) South of Main Street, Boise's largest downtown plaza, *The Grove,* is the site of Alive After Five, a summer concert series that runs on Wed evenings May through Sept.

Continue south across Front Street to access *BoDo,* which features shops and restaurants (plus a hotel and movie multiplex) amid some of the city's oldest warehouses. A new multiple-use complex, *JUMP Boise,* is part community arts center and makers studio, part antique tractor museum, and part headquarters for the J.R. Simplot Company, processor of Idaho potatoes and other food products. JUMP also has a very cool five-story circular slide for kids of all ages.

Boise has a string of parks south of downtown along the Boise River. You could spend several days exploring all the sights of *Julia Davis Park,* where the headliners—all worthy—include the Boise Art Museum, the Idaho Historical Society, Zoo Boise, and the Discovery Center of Idaho (a hands-on kids' museum). The surprise here is the *Idaho Black History Museum* at 508 Julia Davis Dr. Less than 1 percent of Idaho's population is African American, and visitors sometimes wonder whether the state has any blacks at all, but this museum sets the record straight. Located in the former St. Paul's Baptist Church, the museum has featured exhibits on everything from Idaho's jazz heritage to the history of the state's African Americans in the military. Admission is by donation. For current hours and more information, call (208) 789-2164 or see ibhm.org.

Boise is also the unexpected home of a moving tribute to one of history's most famous teenagers. The *Idaho Anne Frank Human Rights Memorial* features a life-size statue of Frank, the young diarist who documented her family's efforts to evade the Nazis during the Holocaust. Visitors will also find reflecting ponds, waterfalls, and walls engraved with the full text of the United Nations' Universal Declaration of Human Rights and dozens of quotes from human-rights leaders past and present. The memorial plaza, open all the time, is located behind the Boise Public Library and The Cabin Literary Center and along the Greenbelt.

East of downtown, Warm Springs Avenue is lined with some of Boise's loveliest homes. On the outskirts of downtown, the *Idaho Botanical Garden* at 2355 Old Penitentiary Rd. hosts summer concerts and a popular Winter Garden aGlow event, but its grounds are fun to stroll in every season. Admission is $7 for adults and $5 for seniors and kids. (There's plenty for children to see and do here, including an adventure garden and tree house.) Spring through fall, the gardens are open 9 a.m. to 5 p.m. Mon through Thurs and until 7 p.m.

Boise's Basque Block

Idaho has the nation's highest percentage of people hailing from Euzkadi, or the Basque homeland that straddles the border of Spain and France. Although pockets of Basque culture can be found throughout the state, Boise, by virtue of its size, is the state's Basque capital. A 1-block area of Boise's downtown is an especially rich site of Basque heritage and culture. Take a stroll down Grove Street between Sixth and Capitol for a look at what's known as Boise's **Basque Block.**

Begin at the **Basque Museum and Cultural Center,** at 611 Grove, which has many fascinating exhibits on all aspects of Basque history and culture. Here you can learn, for example, about famous people of Basque heritage, including Simón Bolivar, Francisco Goya, Balboa, and Juan de la Cosa, who served as Columbus's navigator. Another Basque mariner was responsible for guiding Magellan's ship home after the explorer was killed in the Philippines following the first circumnavigation of the globe.

Visitors discover that most Idaho Basques trace their heritage to the province of Vizcaya in the northwest section of the Basque homeland. Here, too, are history lessons about Gernika, Boise's sister city and the ancient Vizcayan capital and spiritual homeland of the Basques. It was the bombings here during the Spanish Civil War of 1936–1939 that inspired Pablo Picasso's *Guernica* painting, one of his most famous. Gernika is also home to an oak tree that symbolizes Basque liberty; a model of the tree and its surroundings sits in the museum. Next door at 607 Grove St., the **Cyrus Jacobs–Uberuaga House** is also part of the museum. Built in 1864, this is the oldest brick building still standing in Boise. It was the site of the city's first indoor bathtub and the wedding of Senator William Borah. The building served as a Basque boardinghouse for much of the twentieth century. The Basque Museum is open from 10 a.m. to 4 p.m. Tues through Fri and from 11 a.m. to 3 p.m. Sat. Admission is $5 for teens and adults, $4 for seniors age 65 and up, and $3 for children ages 6 through 12. Call (208) 343-2671 or see basquemuseum.com for more information.

The Basque Block has several good places to eat and drink, starting with **Gernika Basque Pub and Eatery.** Established in 1991, it sits at the corner of Grove and Capitol. The menu here includes several Basque-inspired dishes, such as a Solomo sandwich (marinated pork loin topped with pimientos and served on a French roll) or a cheese plate accompanied with fresh bread and grapes. Espresso and craft beers are available, too. Gernika is open from lunch until late daily except Sun. The phone number is (208) 344-2175.

It's not Basque, but **Bardenay** at 610 West Grove St. has a claim to fame as the nation's first restaurant distillery, made possible by a specially passed state law in 1999. (There are locations in Eagle and Coeur d'Alene, too.)

The Basque Market at 608 West Grove St. has tapas-style appetizers to stay or go, paella on the patio, wine tastings, cooking classes, and more. See all the offerings at thebasquemarket.com.

At 117 South Sixth St., **Leku Ona**—which means "the good place" in Basque—is a worthy bookend to the Basque Block. Leku Ona features a wide menu of traditional Basque fare, including squid, cod, beef, and lamb. There's also a boardinghouse-style boutique hotel with rooms priced from $65 to $85. Ask for a room away from the noise on Sixth Street. Call (208) 345-6665 or see lekuonaid.com for more information or reservations.

Fri through Sun. Nov through mid-Mar, regular hours are weekdays only from 9 a.m. to 5 p.m., plus added hours for the holiday lights. See idahobotanical garden.org for upcoming events and garden information.

Next door to the gardens, the ***Old Idaho Penitentiary*** housed inmates from 1870 through 1973. More than 13,000 convicts did time behind its gates, including Harry Orchard, who killed former Idaho governor Frank Steunenberg in 1905 in the aftermath of mining unrest in North Idaho, and Lyda Southard, sentenced to the pen in 1921 after she killed her fourth husband (and maybe her previous spouses, too) with a slice of arsenic-laced apple pie. Visitors can tour the Old Pen on their own or with a guide; some guides earlier served as guards or inmates at the facility. The museum also houses the J. Curtis Earl Collection, a treasure trove of historic arms and military memorabilia. The collection, valued at $3 million, is among the largest of its kind. The Old Pen is open seven days a week from 10 a.m. to 5 p.m. Memorial Day to Labor Day. It's open from noon to 5 p.m. the rest of the year, except state holidays. Admission is $6 for adults and teens, $4 for seniors, and $3 for children ages 6 through 12. (Kids under age 6 are admitted free.) For information call (208) 334-2844 or see the Old Penitentiary page at history.idaho.gov.

Bown Crossing, at the end of Park Center Boulevard in southeast Boise, is a newer neighborhood that doubles as a popular after-work hot spot. Stake a spot on the sidewalk at the family-friendly ***Flatbread Neapolitan Pizzeria*** at 3139 South Bown Way, or enjoy steak, sushi, or Sunday brunch at the more adult-oriented ***Tavern at Bown Crossing*** at 3111 South Bown Way. ***Bier:Thirty Bottle & Bistro*** at 3073 South Bown Way is one of Boise's oldest beer-centric bars, still going strong in a city that has gone crazy for craft brews.

The west edge of Boise's downtown is a bit grittier than the east side. Hot spots here include the ever-evolving ***Freak Alley,*** begun in 2002 in the alley between Eighth and Ninth Streets between Bannock and Idaho Streets and now one of the Northwest's largest mural galleries; the ***Record Exchange*** at 1105 West Idaho St., one of the oldest and coolest music shops on the planet, with CDs, vinyl, and frequent in-store cameos by touring bands; ***Pre Funk Beer Bar*** at 1100 West Front St., featuring a few dozen Idaho and regional brews on tap; and—just two doors down at 1114 West Front St.—***Woodland Empire Ale Craft,*** which creates an array of tasty small-batch beverages. This part of town is also a hub for ***Treefort,*** a celebration of indie music and culture held each March. See treefortmusicfest.com.

A few blocks farther west, the area around Grove Street at 15th Street is known as the Linen District. The retro-cool ***Modern Hotel & Bar,*** 1314 West Grove St., provides a suitably hip base camp for exploring Boise, with a cocktail lounge, patio, and rooms starting at about $115. For more information or reservations, call (866) 780-6012 or see themodernhotel.com. The always-jumping **Big City Coffee** at 1416 West Grove St. is a reliable breakfast spot. On your way, don't miss *Bicycle Trio,* a public art installation on the corner of 14th and Grove that features three stationary cycles that make music as people pedal. (A similar, older work, *Homage to the Pedestrian* by Patrick Zentz, uses motion sensors to trigger music on the west side of the Grove plaza.) Also noteworthy: **a'Tavola,** a gourmet market and cafe open daily except Sun at 1515 West Grove St. for breakfast, lunch, and take-away treats. A few blocks southwest, across "The Connector" (I-184), **Payette Brewing Co.** has a big taproom, beer garden, and food trucks near the Boise River at 733 South Pioneer St.

Even as new neighborhoods emerge, Boise's North End will probably always be among the coolest. **Hyde Park,** a historic district at 13th and Eastman Streets, has an especially good selection of places to eat and drink, including **Sun Ray Cafe** with a big patio at 1602 North 13th St. and **Goody's Soda Fountain** at 1502 North 13th St. **Dunia Marketplace** is a delightful fair-trade shop at 1609 North 13th St. with crafts, toys, jewelry, and decorative items from Idaho and around the world.

Camel's Back Park, just north of the Hyde Park neighborhood, has one of Boise's best playgrounds and access to the Hull's Gulch trails for hiking and mountain biking (also accessible via North Eighth Street, which turns into Sunset Peak Road). See ridgetorivers.org for detailed information on recreational opportunities in Boise's Foothills.

Past Camel's Back Park, 13th Street intersects with Hill Road. Hang a right off Hill to reach Bogus Basin Road, the route to Boise's backyard ski resort of the same name, just 16 miles from downtown. In addition to more than fifty downhill runs over 2,600 acres, **Bogus Basin** has a tubing hill with an 800-foot slide and a tow to take tubers back to the top. Ski-lift tickets run from $29 to $59. Two-hour tubing passes cost $12. The ski hill has several runs open nightly in winter, which makes Bogus an after-work hot spot for Boiseans. During the summer months Bogus offers chair rides, hiking, horseback riding, mountain biking, and disc golf. For more information call (208) 332-5100 or see bogusbasin.org.

For a special winter night out, **Bogus Creek Outfitters** offers sleigh rides from the Bogus Basin Nordic center to a cabin in the woods plus a steak dinner and cowboy-style entertainment. Call (208) 278-7000 or see boguscreek.com for reservations. Back near the Hill Road intersection, **Highlands Hollow Brewhouse** at 2455 North Harrison Hollow Lane is the oldest microbrewery in Boise and a popular après-ski destination with live music on Wednesday nights.

Urban Oasis

Ask many Boiseans what they love most about their city, and chances are they'll mention the Boise River **Greenbelt.** More than 20 miles long, this network of paths reaches from Sandy Point Beach east of the city past Glenwood Street in neighboring Garden City. And as the name implies, much of it runs right along the Boise River.

On a warm weekend day, the Greenbelt could hardly be considered off the beaten path since it sometimes seems half the city is out there walking, running, or bicycling. Even then, however, it's possible to lose the crowds by venturing away from the crowded downtown corridors (near the Boise State University campus and Julia Davis and Ann Morrison Parks) to less-traveled sections.

Here are a few special places of note on or near the Greenbelt:

The **Idaho Shakespeare Festival** has performances at dusk most summer evenings. Most people drive here, but the festival grounds at 5657 Warm Springs Ave. are wedged between the Greenbelt and the Boise River, about a half-hour ride from downtown. (Be sure your bike has a light if you're cycling out for a show.) Pack a picnic or buy food, beer, and wine from the onsite Cafe Shakespeare. For information or tickets call (208) 336-9221 or see idahoshakespeare.org.

The **MK Nature Center** is located at 600 South Walnut St., just east of downtown on the north side of the river. The 4.6-acre site helps visitors understand Idaho's diverse environments from wetlands to high desert. The streamside walking trail is accessible from dawn to dusk every day year-round. The visitor center and gift shop are open 9 a.m. to 5 p.m. Tues through Fri and 11 a.m. to 5 p.m. Sat and Sun. Call (208) 334-2225 for more information.

Surf's up in Idaho! The **Boise River Park** offers engineered waves for kayakers and surfers every day at noon on the river between Fairview Avenue and Veterans Memorial Parkway just west of downtown. It's fun to watch, but to try river surfing yourself, the folks at **Corridor Paddle Surf Shop** at 314 East 35th St. offer advice and rent boards and wetsuits. Additional information can be found at boiseriverpark.com and surf boise.com. For more information on the Boise River Greenbelt, search for it at parks .cityofboise.org, call (208) 608-7600, or visit the Boise Parks & Recreation Department at 1104 Royal Blvd., right along the river near Ann Morrison Park.

The Rest of the Treasure Valley

If Boise is the City of Trees, the communities to its west are its fast-growing branches. Onetime farm towns like Meridian, Star, Eagle, and Kuna have become full-fledged suburbs, while the cities of Nampa and Caldwell form a mini-metropolis of their own. Even outlying towns stretching to the Oregon border have become bedroom communities for Boise and its suburbs. We'll explore the area in counterclockwise fashion from Boise's western city limits.

Nearly surrounded by Boise, Garden City is a 4-square-mile enclave along the Boise River where Chinese immigrants tended food plots that eventually gave the town its name. (The main thoroughfare in Garden City, Chinden Boulevard, combines the words "Chinese" and "garden.") Long known for its used-car lots and cheap motels, Garden City these days is an extension of Boise's bohemian west end. The **Visual Arts Collective** at 3638 Osage St. (a block north of Chinden) is a gallery open on Saturday afternoons and occasional live performance space. Check hours and events at visualartscollective.com. **Telaya Wine Co.,** one of the best-rated in the state, has a tasting room at 240 East 32nd St., open from noon to 6 p.m. daily near the banks of the Boise River.

Garden City also is home to the **Western Idaho Fair,** the state's biggest, held in late August each year. Next to the fairgrounds, the **Boise Hawks** play Northwest League Class A minor-league baseball from mid-June through Labor Day weekend. Games start around 7 p.m., and Memorial Stadium is a fine place to watch the summer sun go down over the Boise Foothills.

Meridian, a booming suburb of about 75,000 people, has two faces: the rampant commercial development along I-84 and its feeder roads, and the much slower pace of an old-time downtown centered around Main Street and Pine Avenue. There are several great places to check out in this haven away from the freeway bustle. One of Meridian's longtime standouts is **Epi's— A Basque Restaurant** in an old house at 1115 North Main St. Squid rolls, shrimp, crab cakes, and lamb loin chops are among the tasty items on the menu. It's open Tues through Sat for dinner. Call (208) 884-0142 for more information or reservations. Another local favorite, **Rick's Press Room,** features upscale yet casual Idaho-inspired food, like a generous slice of salmon sandwiched between mashed potatoes and a hash-brown-like topping that Guy Fieri of the Food Network proclaimed to be "off the hook." True to the restaurant's name, Rick's decor features historic newspaper front pages. Rick's is open for lunch Tues through Fri and dinner Tues through Sat. Find it at 130 East Idaho St. in downtown Meridian and on the Web at rickspressroom.net. The phone number is (208) 288-0558.

North of Meridian and west of Boise, the all-American town of Eagle has a small downtown along State Street. Historic signs tell tales of key buildings including the former Eagle Drug Store at 50 East State St., run for decades by Orville Jackson, who promised to never be "just out" of whatever you needed. (The store is now a bar, one of several interesting spots to eat and drink in the vicinity.) For more local lore, pop into the **Eagle Historical Museum** at 67 East State St., open 9 a.m. to 6 p.m. Tues through Sat.

Three miles west of Eagle via State Street or Highway 44, **Eagle Island State Park** is one of only two state parks in the Boise metropolitan area.

(The other is Lucky Peak, out Warm Springs Road east of Boise. Neither park allows camping.) Eagle Island offers a swimming area with a waterslide, riverside walking paths, and more than 5 miles of trails for horseback riding. It is located at 165 South Eagle Island Pkwy., off Linder Road west of Eagle. Park admission is $5 per vehicle per day. For more information call (208) 939-0696 or see parksandrecreation.idaho.gov/parks/eagle-island.

Highway 16 heads north from US 26 or ID 44 toward Emmett, where the foothills outside town provide a striking location for **Frozen Dog Digs.** This oddly named bed-and-breakfast inn is run by former English teacher and technical writer Jon Elsberry, who has put his personality into the place. Six guest rooms are moderately priced and include a full gourmet breakfast. For reservations or more information, call (208) 365-7372 or see frozendogdigs.com.

On fine autumn days—which includes most of them in Southwestern Idaho—the towns of New Plymouth, Fruitland, and Payette make a great scenic-drive destination. Watch for roadside markets piled with fat orange pumpkins and tart, crisp apples, and stock up on some tasty seasonal produce while enjoying some of the state's loveliest fall foliage. Payette was the hometown of baseball great Harmon Killebrew, who is buried in Riverside Cemetery. Killebrew's 2011 obituary in the *Argus Observer* from nearby Ontario, Oregon, reported that as a small-town kid, "the first major league baseball game Harmon saw was the first one he played in," for the Washington Senators in 1954. He moved with the team to Minnesota in 1960 and played for the Twins until 1974 (plus a year with the Kansas City Royals at the end of his career). Killebrew was a thirteen-time All Star and six-time American League home run champ.

Weiser, located north of Payette, also has a baseball claim to fame: It was here that a young Kansas-born pitcher named Walter "Big Train" Johnson drew the notice of scouts while playing semi-pro ball in the summer of 1907 for the Weiser Kids. Johnson logged twenty-one seasons with the Washington Senators and still holds the major-league record for shutouts, with 110.

A field at the local sports complex honors Johnson, but these days Weiser is best known as the site of the annual **National Oldtime Fiddlers Contest.** As much a family reunion as a competition, the fiddle fests have been going on in Weiser since 1914. The town became host to the Northwest Mountain Fiddlers Contest in 1953, and the national championship was inaugurated in 1963, Idaho's territorial centennial. The contest is held the third full week of June, drawing about 300 contestants of all ages and more than 10,000 spectators. For more information on the contest, call (208) 414-0525 or see fiddlecontest.com.

Chocoholics, don't miss a stop at **Weiser Classic Candy** at 449 State St. in Weiser for hand-dipped chocolates and homemade candies that are shipped nationwide and even around the world. In addition to its tempting candy counter, Weiser Classic Candy serves muffins, bagels, coffee, ice cream, soups, and sandwiches. The shop is open daily except Sun for lunch and afternoon treats. Call (208) 414-2850 or see weiserclassiccandy.com.

North of Weiser, it's a short drive on US 95 through Midvale to Cambridge and the southern gateway to Hells Canyon, covered earlier in this chapter, so we'll continue south on US 95 to visit the southern part of the Treasure Valley.

The small town of Parma is home to a replica of the Hudson's Bay Company's **Fort Boise,** built in 1834 and one of two nineteenth-century forts so named. (The town of Boise grew up around the other, a US Army cavalry post erected in 1863.) The original Fort Boise was situated on the east bank of the Snake River about 8 miles north of the mouth of the Boise River. Although it was built as a fur-trading post, Fort Boise soon switched its emphasis to serving emigrants on the Oregon Trail, and it was a most welcome sight after 300 miles of dry and dusty travel from Fort Hall.

Flooding extensively damaged Fort Boise in 1853, and historians believe any attempts to rebuild it were probably thwarted by increasingly hostile relationships with the Shoshone Indians. Tensions culminated with the 1854 Ward Massacre, in which eighteen emigrants (out of a party of twenty) died; a monument marking the event may be seen in a park south of Middleton, Idaho. Hudson's Bay Company abandoned Fort Boise two years later, and the land on which it originally stood is now a state wildlife management area.

The Fort Boise Replica in Parma sits 5 miles southeast of the original fort site. In addition to the emigrant story, the Fort Boise Replica has artifacts and displays from Southwestern Idaho history. One room features a desk built in 1891 by a boy whose family was traveling to Oregon when their money ran out and they decided to stay. Other exhibits tell how Parma is the only Idaho town to have produced two Gem State governors—Clarence Baldridge, a Republican, and Ben Ross, a Democrat—and how *Tarzan* author Edgar Rice Burroughs spent time here, too, apparently even serving on the city council. The Fort Boise Replica is open from 1 to 3 p.m. Fri, Sat, and Sun during June, July, and Aug. The park adjacent to the fort replica includes a small campground with showers and a dump station, as well as shady picnic spots and a playground.

A statue and historical marker on the Fort Boise grounds also are worth noting. They tell of Marie Dorian, an Iowa Indian married to Pierre Dorian who came to the area with Wilson Price Hunt's party of Astorians in 1811. Three years later Marie and her two children were the sole survivors of a midwinter battle with Bannock Indians at a nearby fur-trading post. They set out with two horses on a 200-mile journey through deep snow and after three months were finally rescued by a Columbia River band of Walla Walla Indians in April.

Parma celebrates its role in pioneer history each June with the Old Fort Boise Days celebration, and the town is also home to one of Idaho's remaining drive-in movie theaters, the *Parma Motor Vu,* which these days hosts occasional wine-tasting events, too. See showtimes at parmamotorvu.com.

Caldwell got its start as a railroad town, and it's an interesting stop for Idaho history buffs. Dearborn Street—1 block south of Cleveland Boulevard (Caldwell's main drag)—is the center of the *Steunenberg Residential Historic District,* packed with old homes reflecting many architectural styles. The southeast corner of Dearborn and 16th Street was the site of the 1905 assassination of former Idaho governor Frank Steunenberg. The historic district is within walking distance of the lovely campus of the College of Idaho, a small liberal-arts school. Caldwell has done a nice job reviving Indian Creek through its downtown area and creating a five-acre park along the waterway.

Warm days, cool nights, and rich soil make valleys along the Snake River just right for growing wine grapes. *Ste. Chapelle* at 19348 Lowell Rd. near Caldwell is among Idaho's oldest and best known wineries. The namesake of a medieval landmark in France, Ste. Chapelle's tasting room is open daily Mar through Oct, and the grounds are the site of a popular summer concert series. (See the lineup at stechapelle.com.) *Sawtooth Winery,* at 13750 Surrey Lane south of Nampa, is also worth a stop for its panoramic view and farm-to-fork dinners. The tasting room is open Wed through Sun. See more info at saw toothwinery.com. *Bitner Vineyards* at 16645 Plum Rd. is a lighthearted place with two bed-and-breakfast rooms tucked away next to the winery, which is open Fri through Sun afternoons or by appointment. See bitnervineyards.com.

Long the second-largest city in Idaho, Nampa is now locked in competition with Meridian for that role. Nampa's downtown is doing well with a

Raise a Glass in Idaho

Like its Northwestern neighbors of Washington and Oregon, the Gem State has embraced fermented grapes and grains, with growing numbers of craft breweries, wineries, and even distilleries. Idaho now has more than fifty *wineries*, with the largest concentration in the Sunny Slope area southwest of Caldwell. The Snake River Valley was designated as Idaho's first American Viticultural Area in 2007. Since then the Eagle Foothills AVA was designated in 2015 and the Lewis-Clark Valley AVA was recognized in 2016.

For coverage of Idaho's burgeoning adult beverage scene (which also includes growing numbers of craft breweries and distilleries), look for copies of the *208 Guide* or see its website at 208guide.com. And for more information on Idaho's wineries, see idahowines.org.

new-in-2015 library and legions of intriguing locally owned businesses, plus outposts of Boise favorites. *Flying M Coffee Garage* at 1314 Second St. South doubles as one of the most interesting live music venues in Idaho, with a steady stream of indie bands stopping by on the long drive between Salt Lake City and Portland. Check upcoming gig listings at flyingmcoffee.com/music. Also noteworthy are *Puffy Mondaes* at 200 12th Ave. South, a wonderful art studio and supply depot, and the *Yesteryear Shoppe* at 1211 First St. South, a huge used bookstore that's one of the best in Idaho. In addition to recent used books of all sorts, Yesteryear stocks rare volumes, vintage vinyl record albums, and other treasures from decades gone by. Beware: It's easy to lose all track of time in the stacks here.

For food, *Brick 29 Bistro* is a good bet for casual fine dining in downtown Nampa. The theme here is "comfort food reinvented," so look for upscale twists on macaroni and cheese, burgers, and soups. Find Brick 29 at 320 11th Ave. South. It's open for lunch Mon through Fri, dinner Mon through Sat, and Sun brunch. Call (208) 468-0029 for more info. *Messenger Pizza* at 1224 First St. South is open daily with creative pies, sandwiches, and beer. The *Nampa Farmers' Market* is downtown, too, with local produce on sale from 9 a.m. to 1 p.m. each Sat from May through Oct.

Also in Nampa, the *Warhawk Air Museum* focuses on World War II history in the air and on land and sea. Aside from a great collection of vintage aircraft, uniforms, and home-front memorabilia, the museum runs a Veteran's History Project that collects and preserves video interviews with Americans— military and civilian—who served during wartime. The museum is at 201 Municipal Way, near the local airport, and it's open daily except Mon. Call (208) 465-6446 for details or see warhawkairmuseum.org.

Budget travelers, international vagabonds, and others who want inexpensive or nontraditional accommodations in the Boise metro area will enjoy *A Country Place–Hostel Boise.* The hostel is in a rural setting at 17322 Can Ada Rd., about 2 miles north of I-84 exit 38. Facilities include a kitchen, barbecue grill, common area, covered patio, big yard, and free wireless Internet access. There are dorm-style hostel beds for $25 plus two private rooms, one with its own bathroom, from $45 for one person or $55 for two. It's a good option for larger families or groups of up to fifteen people, and there's also space for an RV outside. From the hostel, it's about a fifteen-minute drive to Boise. Travelers coming via Greyhound will want to get off the bus in Nampa, not Boise, and take a cab. Get more information by calling (208) 467-6858 or at hostelboise.com. The innkeepers here also own the Trailhead Hostel near Cambridge on the Weiser River Trail.

The Snake River Canyon in Southwestern Idaho is home to the world's largest concentration of nesting eagles, hawks, and prairie falcons. There are two ways to discover this raptor kingdom: tour the ***Morley Nelson Snake River Birds of Prey National Conservation Area*** and visit the ***Peregrine Fund's World Center for Birds of Prey*** near Boise.

The conservation area includes about 485,000 acres along 81 miles of the river, with a short trail and observation area at Dedication Point, best reached via the Swan Falls Road south of Kuna. Visitors may catch a glimpse of raptors soaring through the canyon or nesting in its cracks, crevices, and ledges. Early morning and late afternoon mid-March through mid-June are the best times to visit. Bring binoculars, a bird field guide, water and food, sunscreen, a jacket, and a hat. Search for more information on the conservation area at blm.gov/id, or stop by the BLM offices in Boise (at 3948 Development Ave. near the Boise Airport) or Marsing (at 20 First Ave. West) for maps and a visitor guide.

Because the birds can be difficult to see from the rim, many people take a guided trip on the Snake River, which the BLM allows in the protected area only a few times a year. ***Idaho Guide Service*** runs one- and two-day scenic floats (with no white water) to this area each spring, as well as longer, more rugged trips to the nearby Owyhee River Canyonlands of southwest Idaho, Nevada, and Oregon. See idahoguideservice.com for dates and details.

Scientists study raptors because, like humans, they are near the top of the food chain—and what happens to them could very well happen to us. By the 1970s, the peregrine falcon (for which the Peregrine Fund is named) had almost been wiped out in the United States. But scientists learned that falcons ate smaller birds that had in turn ingested insects exposed to DDT, and the chemical made the falcons' eggshells so thin that the baby birds could not survive.

DDT is now banned in the United States, and the peregrine falcon has made an impressive comeback on our continent. But the chemical remains used in some other nations; that fact, coupled with other environmental woes, has endangered or threatened nearly a quarter of the world's 300 raptor species. So the Peregrine Fund continues to study birds of prey and their status as environmental indicators, and much of this fascinating and important work takes place at the World Center for Birds of Prey and its Velma Morrison Interpretive Center, sitting high on a windswept hill south of Boise. Take I-84 exit 50 and drive 6 miles south to 5668 West Flying Hawk Lane.

Visitors to the center can walk around on their own or join a guided tour. Through films, lectures, and displays, visitors learn how the Peregrine Fund breeds raptors in captivity, then sets them free in their natural habitat. The odds against survival can be high: All peregrines, whether captive bred or born in the wild, face a 50 percent mortality rate during their first year of life. Another 20 percent die in their second year. But those who survive two years usually go on to live an average of fifteen years. At the end of each tour, visitors are often treated to a visit with a live falcon. The World Center for Birds of Prey is open daily except Mon from 10 a.m. to 5 p.m. Mar through Oct and from 10 a.m. to 4 p.m. the rest of the year. Admission is $7 for adults, $6 for senior citizens age 62 and up, and $5 for children ages 4 through 16. Call (208) 362-8687 for more information or see peregrinefund.org.

The Owyhee Outback

Owyhee County deserves its own section in any book about Idaho's lesser-known places, simply for its sheer size and remoteness. It isn't Idaho's biggest county—Idaho County takes that honor with 8,497 square miles. But Owyhee County, tucked into the state's corner, is mostly unexplored and unknown. At 7,643 square miles and with fewer than 11,500 people, it's larger than New Jersey, which has nearly 9 million residents.

It's no surprise, then, that natural attractions rule in this corner of the state. While in Marsing, look for **Lizard Butte,** the volcanic formation looming over town from across the Snake River. Waterfall lovers may wish to travel west of Marsing to see **Jump Creek Falls.** The falls, a silver ribbon cascading into a placid pool, are part of the Bureau of Land Management's Jump Creek Special Recreation Management Area, an area of desert plateau and canyonlands. To get there, head west of Marsing on Highway 55. A mile and a half past the intersection of US 95, turn left onto Cemetery Road. Turn left at the T-intersection with the stop sign and follow Jump Creek Road to the south and the trailhead.

Givens Hot Springs, 12 miles south of Marsing via state Highway 78, got its start as a campground on the Oregon Trail. Pioneers frequently stopped here to wash their clothes; one emigrant said the water was "sufficiently hot to boil eggs." Before that, Native Americans used the area as a base camp. Milford and Martha Givens, pioneers themselves, had seen the springs on their way west. Once they got where they were going, however, they decided they liked Idaho better and came back.

The first Givens Hot Springs bathhouse was built way back in the 1890s, and a hotel stood on the grounds for a while as well. Givens Hot Springs is still a campground, with an enclosed year-round swimming pool, private baths, picnic grounds, softball and volleyball play areas, horseshoe pits, cabins, and RV camping. For more information call (208) 495-2000 or see givenshotsprings.com.

Murphy, a blink-or-you'll-miss-it town on Highway 78, is the seat of Owyhee County. It's also home to the **Owyhee County Museum,** featuring displays of early county artifacts ranging from Native American tools to cowboy gear. Visitors also learn about life in the early mining towns, seen from several perspectives including that of the many Chinese miners who lived and worked in Idaho during the nineteenth century. The museum is open from 10 a.m. to 4 p.m. Tues through Sat year-round. Admission is by donation. Call (208) 495-2319 for more information or current operating hours.

If you enjoy old mining towns but find most far too bustling for your tastes, don't miss *Silver City.* Although fairly well-known, Silver, as the locals call it, is decidedly off the beaten path; it is an often rough and winding 23-mile drive southwest of Highway 78. Look for the sign and War Eagle Mines historical marker near milepost 34 east of Murphy, and drive carefully. The road is generally open from Memorial Day through late October.

Tucked away in the Owyhee Mountains, Silver was a rollicking place from 1864 through the early 1900s. Not only was it county seat for a vast reach of territorial southern Idaho, Silver was also home to the territory's first telegraph and the first daily newspaper. Telephones were in use by the 1880s, and the town was electrified in the 1890s. Silver City had its own doctors, lawyers, merchants . . . even a red-light district. During its heyday the town had a population of 2,500 people and seventy-five businesses, all made possible by the fabulous riches on War Eagle Mountain.

All this seems unlikely—even unbelievable—today. Silver City isn't technically a ghost town, because about sixty families maintain part-time residences in the vicinity. But there are just a handful of telephones to the outside world; within town, about two dozen more run on the town's magneto crank system, reportedly the last in Idaho. There's no local mail delivery and no electricity. It's not even the county seat anymore, since that honor went to Murphy in 1934. (The Idaho legislature finally made the change official in 1999.) Needless to say, there's no gas station, either.

Silver City's charm is that it has barely enough amenities to make an overnight or weekend stay possible, yet it hasn't become nearly as commercialized as many other Western "ghost towns." The best way to enjoy Silver is simply to walk its dusty streets, survey the many interesting buildings, and try to imagine what life was like here more than a hundred years ago. The second weekend after Labor Day marks the town's open house, when about ten buildings not normally open to the public may be seen for a nominal fee. Proceeds help pay the town watchman. The Fourth of July is another fun, but busy and crowded, time, with family activities including a parade and games. If you want solitude, you'd be better off visiting another time.

The *Idaho Hotel* serves as Silver City's focal point. Gorgeous antiques—an ice chest, slot machine, and pianos—vie for attention with whimsical signs and racks of guidebooks. The hotel was originally built in nearby Ruby City in 1863 and moved to Silver in 1866. Although many visitors simply stop in for a cold drink, short-order meal, books, or postcards, it's still possible to stay overnight in the Idaho Hotel. Rates range from $80 to $210 per room. The hotel can also provide full family-style meals, with about a week's advance notice, to nonguests as well as guests.

The Empire Room may be the inn's finest. Used on occasion as a honeymoon suite, it is named for the style in which it is furnished, with some pieces dating from the Late Empire era of the 1840s. Woodstoves provide heat, and kerosene and twelve-volt lamps shed light. The bedrooms are too small and historic to accommodate full baths, so there are toilets, sinks, and showers in other rooms down the hallways.

Rooms in the Idaho Hotel are available from Memorial Day until mid-October; after that, the city water system is turned off for the winter. Reservations are advised. For more information from May through October, call (208) 583-4104 or see the hotel's page at historicsilvercityidaho.com, a good online source of information about town services and events. In the off-season, you can call (208) 863-4768 for information. The Bureau of Land Management also has a small campground at Silver City, and its sites are free.

Back on Highway 78 watch for the signs to Oreana. Located in a scenic valley 2 miles south of the highway, Oreana has a population of seven, maybe eight, according to the sign at the "city limits." It's also the setting for ***Our Lady, Queen of Heaven Catholic Church,*** a striking stone building that started life as a general store. Mike Hyde, an area rancher, built the store from native stone in the late 1800s. When only its walls were completed, word was heard around Oreana that a war party of Indians was on its way to the town. All the local folks reportedly took refuge behind the stone walls, expecting an attack. But the Boise-based militia arrived first, and the Indians were deterred.

The store served the Oreana area well into the twentieth century, but by 1961 it had been empty and unused for some time. That year, Albert Black—on whose land it stood—gave the old building to the Catholic Diocese in Nampa. The diocese encouraged local Catholics to turn the store into a church, and Our Lady, Queen of Heaven, was the result. The small belfry atop the church houses the bell that originally hung at Our Lady of Tears in Silver City. The bell survived a 1943 flood and still rings to herald occasional services at the church. Unfortunately the church is not open for tours, but it's still worth a look from the outside if you're in the area. Masses are held several times a year. Call St. Paul's Parish church in Nampa at (208) 466-7031 for dates.

Snake River Vistas

Near the Owyhee-Elmore County line, just outside the town of Grand View, Jack and Belva Lawson have created one of the state's most unusual tourist attractions at **Lawson's EMU-Z-Um.** Here, on the land they've worked since 1967, the Lawsons have set up a replica of an 1860s town, complete with the contents of the Silver City Schoolhouse Museum. Visitors also see a silver mine replica, model trains, pioneer and Native American artifacts, and one of the area's first hand-built automobiles.

EMU-Z-Um—it got its name from the emus the Lawsons raise—is open from 9 a.m. to 5 p.m. Fri through Sun, Mar 1 through Oct 15, with weekday and winter visits by appointment. Admission is $10 for ages 13 and up and $5 for children ages 6 to 12. Bring a picnic lunch and plan to spend some time; there's a lot to see. To get there, look for the sign between mile markers 52 and 53 on Highway 78. For more information see emuzum.com. To make an off-season appointment, call the Lawsons at (208) 834-2397.

Mountain Home, 23 miles from Grand View via Highway 67, is an Air Force town and a popular stop for travelers on I-84. Few visitors make it past the clot of gas stations and restaurants at exit 95, but those who do will find a few interesting places in town.

The military's presence is unmistakable in Mountain Home: Look no farther than **Carl Miller Park,** possibly the only place in the United States where you can picnic in the shadow of an F-111 fighter jet. The park was established in 1919 as a memorial for the first local soldier killed in World War I. This is also the site of Mountain Home's annual Air Force Appreciation Days, held the Fri and Sat after Labor Day weekend each year. Thousands of people turn out annually for the parade, free barbecue, and other events.

Mountain Home also has a growing collection of murals, mostly done by local artist Randall Miller. The largest, 49 feet by 8 feet, is on the side of the NAPA Auto Parts store at 295 East Jackson St. It depicts Commodore Jackson, who staked a claim on what would become the Mountain Home town site in the 1880s. Miller also created a mural out of thousands of pennies on the wall outside Kurly's Sports Bar & Grill at 124 East Jackson St.

Mountain Home is the main gateway for trips to **Anderson Ranch Reservoir** and the **Trinity Lakes** area. Anderson Reservoir dams the South Fork of the Boise River, and while the human-made lake isn't especially scenic, it does have plenty of inlets and bays that provide visual relief from the high-and-dry hills all around. Fuel up in Mountain Home, because there are few services at Anderson Ranch Reservoir and none at Trinity Lakes.

At a pretty cove on the northwest side of the reservoir 8 miles from the dam, **Fall Creek Resort and Marina** offers eleven rooms priced at $75 and up for double occupancy, which includes use of a sauna, hot tub, and exercise equipment. Other amenities include a restaurant and lounge; kayak, paddleboard, and pedal boat rentals; and an RV park. Call (208) 653-2242 for more information. From Fall Creek north it's 17 miles to Trinity Mountain. (Take Forest Service Roads 123 and 129.) The steep, rough route is passable by most vehicles, but forget towing a trailer. For a much easier route to the Trinity Lakes region, choose the Pine-Featherville Road, accessed off US Highway 20, then follow the signs to Trinity Lakes via Forest Service Road 172. It's a bit farther "as the crow flies," but it'll save a lot of wear and tear on your car or truck.

If the scenery was ho-hum around Anderson Reservoir, it is sublime in the highlands at Trinity Lakes. Stake a spot at one of four campgrounds (which charge about $10 a night, first come, first served), or rent one of two Forest Service cabins via recreation.gov. (Search for Big Trinity Cabin.)

Not surprisingly the Trinity Lakes region is popular with anglers and hikers. The 4-mile, pedestrians-only *Rainbow Basin Trail* takes trekkers into a subalpine cirque basin dotted with nine lakes and populated by lots of critters including elk, deer, mountain lion, and black bear. From Trinity Mountain you can backtrack to Anderson Ranch Reservoir or travel the rough Forest Service roads to Atlanta (see the Boise Basin section).

Southeast of Mountain Home, the top attraction is *Bruneau Dunes State Park.* Most sand dunes form at the edge of a natural basin, but these form at the center, making them unique in the Western Hemisphere. The Bruneau complex also includes the largest single structured sand dune in North America, with its peak 470 feet high. The combination of sand and a natural trap has caused sand to collect here for about 15,000 years, and the prevailing wind patterns—from the southeast 28 percent of the time and from the northwest 32 percent—ensure the dunes don't move far. The two prominent dunes cover about 600 acres.

Hiking, camping, and fishing are favorite activities at the Bruneau Dunes. Hiking to the top of a sand dune is an experience unlike any other. Once there, many hikers simply linger a while to savor the view before walking the crest of the dunes back to terra firma. Others use the dunes' inside bowl for sledding, sand skiing, or snowboarding. Bass and bluegill thrive in the small lakes at the foot of the dunes, and the campground—with one of the longest seasons in Idaho—has a steady stream of visitors March through late fall. Bruneau Dunes State Park has a good visitor center featuring displays of wildlife and natural history. There's also an observatory that features astronomy programs at dusk Fri and Sat evenings, spring through fall. Take I-84 exit 95 or 112 to the dunes. A $5-per-vehicle park entrance fee is charged, and observatory programs are $5 per person for everyone over age five. For more information call (208) 366-7919 or see parksandrecreation.idaho.gov/parks/bruneau-dunes.

At what is now *Three Island Crossing State Park,* pioneers traveling west on the Oregon Trail faced the most difficult river crossing of their 2,000-mile journey. Many chose not to ford the river and continued along the south bank of the Snake River through the same country we've just traversed. But about half the emigrants decided to brave the Snake to the shorter, easier route on the river's north side. It's still possible to see the islands used in the crossing, as well as scars worn by the wagon wheels. See exhibits about the arduous trek at the park's year-round Oregon Trail History and Education Center. Recreational activities include camping, fishing, swimming, disc golf, and picnicking. Eight camping cabins rent for $50 each, and there's a popular RV and tent camp-ground, too, so it's best to reserve a spot. Three Island Crossing State Park is reached via exit 120 off of I-84. Drive south into Glenns Ferry and follow the signs to the park. For more information call (208) 366-2394 or check out parks andrecreation.idaho.gov/parks/three-island-crossing.

Right next door to the state park, the vineyards at *Crossings Winery* date to the 1980s, making them some of Idaho's oldest. Once known as Carmela Winery, Crossings occupies a building that looks like a hybrid of medieval castle and French chateau. In addition to a tasting room that's open daily from 10 a.m. to 8 p.m. and a well-regarded restaurant, Tannins (open daily for lunch and dinner), Crossings has its own golf course. Greens fees are $16 for nine holes and $25 for eighteen holes, with carts available and discounts for service members and senior golfers. If Three Island's campground is full, try Crossings' RV park. The business also rents cabins that are fancier than those at the state park for about $100 a night. For more information call (208) 366-2313 or see crossingswinery.com.

Places to Stay in Southwestern Idaho

MCCALL

America's Best Value Inn & Suites
415 North Third St.
(208) 634-6300
americasbestvalueinn
mccall.com
Moderate

Hotel McCall
1101 North Third St.
(866) 800-1183
hotelmccall.com
Moderate–Expensive

The Hunt Lodge–Holiday Inn Express
210 North Third St.
(208) 634-4700
thehuntlodge.com
Moderate–Expensive

Scandia Inn Motel
401 North Third St.
(208) 634-7394
thescandiainn.com
Inexpensive–Moderate

Shore Lodge
501 West Lake St.
(800) 657-6464
shorelodge.com
Moderate–Expensive

NEW MEADOWS

Hartland Inn & Motel
Highway 55 and US 95
(208) 347-2114
thehartlandinn.com
Inexpensive–Moderate

Meadows Valley Motel
302 North Norris St.
(208) 347-2175
meadowsvalleymotel.com
Inexpensive

COUNCIL

Elkhorn Bed & Breakfast
Six miles north of town on US 95
(208) 256-4556
elkhornbnb.com
Moderate

CAMBRIDGE

Cambridge House
95 South First St.
(208) 257-3555
Moderate

Frontier Motel & RV Park
240 South Superior St.
(208) 257-3851
Inexpensive

Mundo Hot Springs
3024 Goodrich Rd.
(208) 257-3849
mundohotsprings.com
Inexpensive–Moderate

MIDVALE

Trailhead Guesthouse and Hostel
(208) 473-6292
trailheadhostel.com
Inexpensive

YELLOW PINE

Yellow Pine Lodge
(208) 633-3377
Inexpensive

WARM LAKE

North Shore Lodge
(208) 632-2000
northshorelodgeidaho.com
Inexpensive–Moderate

DONNELLY

Boulder Creek Inn & Suites
629 Highway 55
(208) 325-8638
thebouldercreekinn.com
Moderate

Long Valley Motel
161 South Main St.
(208) 325-8271
Inexpensive

Tamarack Resort
311 Village Dr.
(west side of Lake Cascade)
(208) 325-1000
tamarackidaho.com
Moderate–Expensive

CASCADE

Alpine Lodge & Motel & RV Park
900 South US 95
(208) 382-4948
alpinelodgemotel.com
Inexpensive–Moderate

Ashley Inn
500 North Main St.
(208) 382-5621
theashleyinn.com
Expensive

Birch Glen Lodge & Motel
762 South Main St.
(208) 382-4238
birchglenlodge.com
Inexpensive–Moderate

GARDEN VALLEY/ CROUCH

Terrace Lakes Resort
101 Holiday Dr.
(208) 462-3250
terracelakes.com
Inexpensive–Moderate

LOWMAN

Sourdough Lodge & RV Resort
(208) 259-3326
sourdoughlodge.com
Inexpensive–Moderate

GRANDJEAN

Sawtooth Lodge
(208) 259-3331
sawtoothlodge.com
Moderate

IDAHO CITY

Idaho City Hotel
215 Montgomery St.
(208) 392-4499
idahocityhotel.net
Inexpensive

A One Step Away Bed & Breakfast
112 Cottonwood St.
(208) 392-4938
aonestepaway.com
Inexpensive–Moderate

ATLANTA

Beaver Lodge
(208) 864-2132
beaverlodgeatlanta.com
Inexpensive

BOISE

Best Western Vista Inn
2645 Airport Way
(208) 336-8100
bestwestern.com
Moderate

Boise Guest House
614 North Fifth St.
(208) 761-6798
boiseguesthouse.com
Moderate–Expensive

Grove Hotel
245 South Capitol Blvd.
(208) 333-8000
grovehotelboise.com
Expensive

Hampton Inn & Suites
495 South Capitol Blvd.
(208) 331-1900
hamptoninn.com
Expensive

Homewood Suites
7957 West Spectrum Way
(208) 385-8500
homewoodsuites3.hilton.com
Expensive

Hotel 43
981 Grove St.
(208) 342-4622
hotel43.com
Expensive

Inn at 500 Capitol
500 South Capitol Blvd.
(208) 840-1040
innat500.com
Expensive

Leku Ona
117 South Sixth St.
(208) 345-6665
lekuonaid.com
Inexpensive–Moderate

The Modern Hotel
1314 West Grove St.
(208) 424-8244
themodernhotel.com
Moderate–Expensive

MERIDIAN

Bella Vista B&B
4601 South Ramona St.
(208) 866-6012
bellavistaid.com
Moderate

**Best Western Plus
Rama Inn**
1019 South Progress Ave.
(208) 887-7888
bestwestern.com
Moderate

**Mr. Sandman Inn
& Suites**
1575 South Meridian Rd.
(800) 959-2230
mrsandmaninn.com
Moderate

EAGLE

Hilton Garden Inn
145 East Riverside Dr.
(208) 938-9600
hiltongardeninn3.hilton
.com
Expensive

EMMETT

**Frozen Dog Digs Bed &
Breakfast**
4325 Frozen Dog Rd.
(208) 365-7372
frozendogdigs.com
Moderate–Expensive

Holiday Motel & RV Park
1111 South Washington
Ave.
(208) 365-4479
holidaymotelandrv.com
Moderate

WEISER

Colonial Motel
251 East Main St.
(208) 549-0150
colonialmotel.us
Inexpensive

**Indianhead Motel
& RV Park**
747 US 95
(208) 549-0331
Inexpensive

CALDWELL

**Bitner Vineyards Bed
& Breakfast**
16645 Plum Rd.
(208) 455-1870
bitnervineyards.com
Expensive

**Canyon Springs
RV Resort**
21965 Chicago Ave.
(208) 402-6630
canyonspringsrvresort.com
Moderate

La Quinta Inn
901 Specht Ave.
(208)454-2222
lq.com
Moderate

NAMPA

**A Country Place–Hostel
Boise**
17322 Can Ada Rd.
(208) 467-6858
hostelboise.com
Inexpensive

Nampa Super 8
624 Nampa Blvd.
(208) 467-2888
Inexpensive–Moderate

Shilo Inn–Nampa Suites
1401 Shilo Dr.
(208) 498-1000
shiloinns.com
Moderate

SILVER CITY

Idaho Hotel
(208) 583-4104
historicsilvercityidaho.com
Moderate

MOUNTAIN HOME

**Best Western Foothills
Motor Inn**
1080 US 20
(208) 587-8477
bestwesternidaho.com
Moderate

Mountain Home Inn
1180 US 20
(208) 587-9743
Moderate

**ANDERSON RANCH
RESERVOIR AREA**

**Fall Creek Resort and
Marina**
(208) 653-2242
fallcreekresortandmarina
.com
Moderate

Nester's Pine Resort and Motel
(208) 653-2210
Inexpensive–Moderate

GLENNS FERRY

Crossings Winery
1294 West Madison St.
(208) 366-2313
crossingswinery.com
Moderate

Redford Motel
525 West First Ave.
(208) 366-2421
Inexpensive

Places to Eat in Southwestern Idaho

MCCALL

FoggLifter Cafe
(American)
1003 North Third St.
(208) 634-5507
Inexpensive

Lardo's Grill & Saloon
(American)
600 West Lake St.
(208) 634-8191
Inexpensive–Moderate

The Mill Supper Club
(American)
324 North Third St.
(208) 634-7683
Moderate

The Pancake House
(American)
209 North Third St.
(208) 634-5849
Inexpensive–Moderate

Pueblo Lindo
(Mexican)
1007 West Lake St.
(208) 634-2270
Inexpensive–Moderate

Rupert's
(Northwest)
1101 North Third St.
(at Hotel McCall)
(208) 634-8108
Moderate–Expensive

CAMBRIDGE

Bucky's Cafe
(American)
US 95
(208) 257-3330
Inexpensive

DONNELLY

Flight of Fancy
(coffeehouse/bakery)
282 North Main St.
(208) 325-4432
Inexpensive

YELLOW PINE

Yellow Pine Lodge
(American)
(208) 633-3377
Inexpensive

WARM LAKE

North Shore Lodge
(American)
(208) 632-2000
Inexpensive–Moderate

CASCADE

Gramma's Family Restaurant
(American)
224 North Main St.
(208) 382-4602
Inexpensive–Moderate

Route 55 Cafe
(family)
806 South Main St.
(208) 382-4496
Inexpensive

GRANDJEAN

Sawtooth Lodge
(American)
(208) 259-3331
Inexpensive–Moderate

IDAHO CITY

Trudy's Kitchen
(American)
419 Highway 21
(208) 392-4151
Inexpensive–Moderate

ATLANTA

Beaver Lodge
(American)
(208) 864-2132
Inexpensive–Moderate

BOISE

Berryhill
(New American)
121 North Ninth St.
(208) 363-7373
Moderate–Expensive

Big City Coffee
(breakfast)
1416 Grove St.
(208) 345-3145
Inexpensive

Cottonwood Grille
(Northwest)
913 West River Dr.
(208) 333-9800
Moderate–Expensive

The Dish
(New American)
205 N. 10th St.
(208) 344-4231
Moderate–Expensive

HELPFUL WEBSITES FOR SOUTHWESTERN IDAHO

Boise Convention & Visitors Bureau
boise.org

Boise Weekly (alternative news and culture)
boiseweekly.com

Idaho Statesman (Boise daily newspaper)
idahostatesman.com

McCall Area Chamber of Commerce & Visitors Bureau
mccallchamber.org

Idaho Press–Tribune (Nampa/Caldwell–area newspaper)
idahopress.com

Mountain Home Chamber of Commerce
mountainhomechamber.localality.com

Even Stevens
(sandwiches and salads)
815 West Bannock St.
(208) 343-4018
Inexpensive

Flatbread Neapolitan Pizzeria
3139 South Bown Way
(208) 343-4177
Inexpensive–Moderate

Fork
(New American)
199 North Eighth St.
(208) 287-1700
Moderate–Expensive

Front Door
(pizza and craft beer)
105 South Sixth St.
(208) 287-9201
Inexpensive–Moderate

Gernika Basque Pub & Eatery
202 South Capitol Blvd.
(208) 344-2175
Inexpensive

Highlands Hollow Brew House
(pub)
2455 Harrison Hollow Lane
(208) 343-6820
Moderate

Leku Ona
(Basque)
117 South Sixth St.
(208) 345-6665
Moderate

Life's Kitchen
(New American)
1025 South Capitol Blvd.
(208) 331-0199
Inexpensive

Red Feather Lounge
(eclectic)
246 North Eighth St.
(208) 343-3119
Moderate–Expensive

Reef
(Island/Northwest)
105 South Sixth St.
(208) 287-9200
Inexpensive–Moderate

Sun Ray Cafe
(pizza/American)
1602 North 13th St.
(208) 343-2887
Inexpensive–Moderate

Tavern at Bown Crossing
(fine dining)
3111 South Bown Way
(208) 345-2277
Moderate–Expensive

MERIDIAN

Epi's
(Basque)
1115 North Main St.
(208) 884-1142
Moderate

Louie's
(Italian)
2500 East Fairview Ave.
(208) 884-5200
Moderate

Rick's Press Room
(Northwest)
130 East Idaho St.
(208) 288-0558
Moderate

EAGLE

Bella Aquila
(Italian)
775 South Rivershore
Lane
(208) 938-1900
Moderate–Expensive

Rib Shack Barbecue
395 West State St.
(208) 938-0008
Inexpensive–Moderate

**Wild West Bakery &
Espresso**
(American)
83 East State St.
(208) 939-5677
Inexpensive–Moderate

WEISER

Idaho Pizza Company
17 West Commercial St.
(208) 549-8765
Inexpensive–Moderate

Weiser Classic Candy
(sandwich shop)
449 State St.
(208) 414-2850
Inexpensive

EMMETT

**Blue Ribbon Cafe &
Bakery**
(American)
515 South Washington
Ave.
(208) 365-3290
Inexpensive

Cold Mountain Creek
(American)
1825 Highway 16
(208) 365-1570
Inexpensive–Moderate

PARMA

Parma Ridge Winery
(New American)
24509 Rudd Rd.
(208) 946-5187
Inexpensive–Moderate
(open Fri–Sun)

CALDWELL

Fiesta Guadalajara
(Mexican)
420 North 10th Ave.
(208) 455-8605
Inexpensive

Hamburger Connection
(American)
423 South 10th Ave.
(208) 454-8477
Inexpensive

Sage Cafe
(American)
2929 Franklin Rd.
(208) 454-2084
Inexpensive–Moderate

NAMPA

Brick 29 Bistro
(New American)
320 11th Ave. South
(208) 468-0029
Moderate–Expensive

**The Dewey Restaurant
& Lounge**
(American)
113 13th Ave. South
(208) 461-3584
Inexpensive–Moderate

The Egg Factory
(breakfast and lunch)
820 Nampa-Caldwell Blvd.
(208) 466-2728
Inexpensive

ALSO WORTH SEEING IN SOUTHWESTERN IDAHO

Zims Hot Springs
New Meadows

Bronco Stadium
Boise State University campus, Boise

**Roaring Springs Water Park/Wahooz
Family Fun Zone**
Meridian

Crooked Fence Brewing
US 16 northwest of Eagle

Hispanic Cultural Center of Idaho
Nampa

**Orma J. Smith Museum of Natural
History**
College of Idaho campus, Caldwell

Messenger Pizza
1224 First Street South
(208) 461-0081
Inexpensive

MARSING

Spot Pizza
12 Sandbar Ave.
(208) 896-5055
Inexpensive–Moderate

MOUNTAIN HOME

Pat's Desert Inn Cafe
(American)
1500 Sunset Strip
(208) 580-9443
Inexpensive

Smoky Mountain Pizzeria Grill
(Italian)
1465 American Legion Blvd.
(208) 587-2840
Inexpensive–Moderate

ANDERSON RANCH RESERVOIR AREA

Deer Creek Lodge
(American)
Pine-Featherville Road
(208) 653-2454
Inexpensive–Moderate

Fall Creek Resort and Marina
(American)
(208) 653-2242
Inexpensive–Moderate

GLENNS FERRY

Crossings Winery
(American)
1289 West Madison Ave.
(208) 366-2313
Moderate–Expensive

South Central Idaho

To the casual traveler along I-84, South Central Idaho seems an arid, apparently barren expanse on the way to somewhere else—most likely Boise or Salt Lake City. To many visitors the best show seems to be in the sky, where clouds roll over wide vistas hemmed by distant mountain peaks.

This big landscape hides its treasures well, but they're not hard to find if you get off the freeway. US 30, a slower and more scenic alternative to I-84, crosses the region from Bliss east to Heyburn (near Burley) before returning to the freeway; Twin Falls, the region's largest city and crossroads to points north and south, is about midway, offering a good beginning and end to loop day trips. From Twin Falls, US 93 drops south over high desert into Nevada, while US 75 climbs north over rugged lava fields to Sun Valley and the rest of mountainous Central Idaho. From these spokes, small byways and farm roads provide the passport to fertile farmland, abundant recreation, and one of the world's great canyons.

For more South Central Idaho travel information, call (800) 255-8946 or see visitsouthidaho.com.

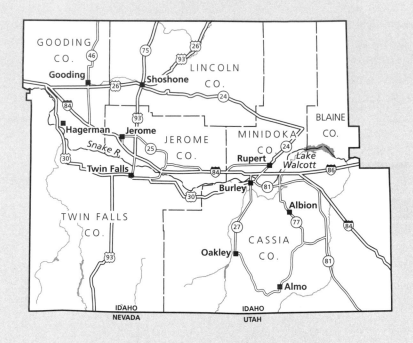

GOODING
CO.

LINCOLN
CO.

Gooding

Shoshone

BLAINE
CO.

Hagerman

Jerome

JEROME
CO.

MINIDOKA
CO.

Rupert

Lake
Walcott

Snake R.

Twin Falls

Burley

Albion

TWIN FALLS
CO.

CASSIA
CO.

Oakley

Almo

IDAHO
NEVADA

IDAHO
UTAH

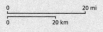

0   20 mi

0   20 km

The Hagerman Valley

In many cases, South Central Idaho's best-kept secrets are just a few miles off the interstate. In the case of Malad Gorge, the highway literally passes right overhead. The Big Wood River and Little Wood River become the Malad River, tumbling into a canyon 250 feet deep and just 140 feet wide at Malad Gorge. This area, called the Devil's Washbowl, is part of **Thousand Springs State Park,** which includes five units near Hagerman. All of them are just a short drive from I-84, but Malad Gorge is the closest, making it a handy spot for a break from the interstate via exit 147 at Tuttle.

Malad is French for "sick," and Malad Gorge got its name when nineteenth-century fur trappers became ill after eating beaver caught nearby. The Malad River itself is thought to be one of the world's shortest, running just 12 miles before being swallowed up by the mighty Snake River downstream. A short trail from the main parking area leads to a footbridge over the plunge. Wagon-wheel ruts from the Kelton Road, an old freight route from Utah to Idaho, may be seen nearby, as may traces of the old stage stop. Park staff discovered these years ago while cleaning up a local garbage dump. Malad Gorge has facilities for hiking and picnicking, but no camping is permitted. The park's roads are excellent for walking, jogging, or bicycling; indeed this is the site of a popular annual run/walk event held the Saturday before each St. Patrick's Day. Most days, however, you'll likely have the place to yourself. For more information on Malad Gorge and the other Thousand Springs State Park units, call (208) 837-4505 or see parksandrecreation.idaho.gov/parks/thousand-springs.

From Malad Gorge it's a short drive to more scenic wonders. Northwest of Gooding via Highway 46, the **Gooding City of Rocks** and **Little City of Rocks** offer panoramas of highly eroded canyon lands, Native American petro-

AUTHOR'S FAVORITES IN SOUTH CENTRAL IDAHO

City of Rocks National Reserve
south of Burley

Herrett Center for Arts and Science
Twin Falls

Shoshone Falls
east of Twin Falls

Snake River Canyon
Twin Falls

The South Hills (Sawtooth National Forest)
south of Hansen

glyphs, and spring wildflowers. Both areas are located west off of Highway 46, and they're particularly appealing to kids, who will have a ball exploring the fantastic rock formations—but keep your eyes open for rattlesnakes and the elk herds who live on the high desert lands nearby. Highway 46 continues north to a sweeping vista of the Camas Prairie, its blue flowers usually in bloom shortly before Memorial Day.

The **Gooding Hotel Bed & Breakfast** is owned by Dean Gooding, the great-great-nephew of former Idaho governor and US senator Frank Gooding, and Dean's wife, Judee. Gooding was an old railroad town, and the hotel is hard by the tracks. Then as now its location was ideal, within walking distance of restaurants, bars, and shops. See room descriptions at goodinghotelbandb .com, then call (208) 934-4374 for current rates and reservations. If you're in Gooding in midsummer, don't miss the annual **Basque Picnic,** usually served the third Sunday of July at the Gooding County Fairgrounds. The event includes a barbecue of lamb chops, chorizo (a highly seasoned pork sausage), beans, rice, and more, plus dancing, music, and games. The Gooding Pro Rodeo takes place here each August, too.

South of Gooding the town of Wendell provides access to both sides of the Snake River Canyon and to the Hagerman Valley, where recreation and relaxation are a way of life. Ritter Island is the centerpiece of a unit of Thousand Springs State Park and the site of one of the state's best arts festivals, held in late September; see thousandspringsfestival.org. There's excellent birdwatching, canoeing, and kayaking nearly year-round. To get there take I-84 exit 155 from Wendell. Turn right and drive 3 miles. Take a left onto 1500 East, drive 2.5 miles, then turn right onto 3200 South. Take this road 2 miles. You will see a sign. Turn right at the sign and then take a quick right.

Hagerman is accessible via US 30 south from Bliss or north from Buhl and via the Vader Grade west from Wendell. With its year-round mild climate and abundant recreation, the heart of the Hagerman Valley offers many pleasures, and it's easy to enjoy several diversions on any given day. Fishing is a major lure, with some of the state's most productive waters—the Snake River, Billingsley Creek, Oster Lakes, and the Anderson Ponds—located nearby. Floating is another popular pastime, on a 10-mile stretch of river where Class 3 rapids alternate with calm stretches. Rafters often can take to the Snake as early as April 1 (and as late as Halloween), with the area just below the Lower Salmon Falls Power Plant the most popular spot to put in. Many people navigate this stretch on their own, but **Idaho Guide Service** offers day trips here for about $70 a person including lunch. See idahoguideservice.com or call (208) 734-4998.

TOP ANNUAL EVENTS IN SOUTH CENTRAL IDAHO

Western Days
Twin Falls (early June)

Idaho Regatta
Burley (last weekend in June)

Twin Falls City Band Concerts
(each Thurs June through early Aug)

Sagebrush Days
Buhl (Fourth of July week)

Gooding Basque Picnic
(third Sunday in July)

Twin Falls County Fair and Magic Valley Stampede
Filer (six days ending Labor Day)

Thousand Springs Festival of the Arts
Hagerman Valley (late Sept)

A float trip below Lower Salmon Falls is the best way to sneak a peek at ***Teater's Knoll,*** the only Idaho structure designed by Frank Lloyd Wright. The home and studio, which are perched high above the Snake, were built for Western artist Archie Teater and his wife, Patricia, who lived there part-time from the late 1950s through the 1970s. The home, later purchased and restored by modern-day Idaho architect Henry Whiting, is on the National Register of Historic Places. It is currently inaccessible to the public.

For a good meal in Hagerman, try the ***Snake River Grill*** at State and Hagerman Streets, open daily for breakfast and lunch and nightly except Mon for dinner. Specialties include catfish, sturgeon, pasta, and wild game. Many locals and day-trippers drop in for the yummy burgers, catfish, and sturgeon, but classically trained chef Kirt Martin also is known for creating feasts with all sorts of wild game brought in by customers. (So now you know what to do with that venison or elk roast your brother-in-law gives you every hunting season. Call 208-837-6227 to make arrangements.)

As if all this wasn't enough to entice visitors to Hagerman, the town is host to an unusual archaeological find. The ***Hagerman Fossil Beds National Monument*** marks the spot where an area farmer discovered fossils that turned out to be those of the zebra-like Hagerman Horse, now the official Idaho state fossil. In the 1930s the Smithsonian Institution sent several expeditions to collect specimens of the horse. Archaeologists unearthed 130 skulls and 15 skeletons of an early, zebra-like horse that dated back to the Pliocene age, about 3.4 million years ago. Other fossils in the area preserved early forms of camel, peccary, beaver, turtle, and freshwater fish.

The monument has a visitor center at 221 North State St. in Hagerman, open from 9 a.m. to 5 p.m. daily in summer and Thurs through Mon the rest of the year. Stop there to see the exhibits and get directions to other monument areas open to the public; opportunities include several hiking trails and interpretive areas. The monument also occasionally has tours and special programs, mostly on Sat in summer. For more information or a schedule, call (208) 933-4105 or see nps.gov/hafo.

South of Hagerman, US 30 enters Twin Falls County. The highway here is known as the *Thousand Springs Scenic Route,* and like the nearby state park, the scenic highway takes its name from the white cascades that gush from the black basalt of the Snake River Canyon. At one time there probably were truly a thousand springs, give or take a few. Today there are far fewer, but the sight remains impressive.

Where do the springs originate? Many have traveled underground from near Arco, where the Big Lost River and several other streams abruptly sink underground. From there the water moves ever so slowly, possibly just 10 feet a day, through the Snake River Aquifer before bursting forth from the canyon walls. In other words, the water you see here entered the aquifer about the year 1800 and has been making its way across the underground aquifer ever since. *Thousand Springs Tours* specializes in scenic floats and lunch and dinner cruises in the area. Call (208) 837-9006 or see 1000springs.com for information and reservations.

Hot springs also are abundant in the area, and several resorts cater to travelers and locals who want an easy staycation. Across from Ritter Island, *1000 Springs Resort* offers indoor swimming year-round in a spacious pool and riverside picnicking and camping. Call (208) 837-4987 or see 1000springs resort.com. *Miracle Hot Springs* and *Banbury Hot Springs,* located on either side of US 30 9 miles south of Hagerman, share ownership. Both offer general-admission pools and private VIP baths and several camping and cabin options, plus massage therapy and watercraft rentals. See miraclehotspring .com for complete hours and rates for both resorts.

South Central Idaho produces a whopping 90 percent of the world's commercially raised trout, and *Clear Springs Foods*—by far the largest of the trout processors—provides a glimpse of the fish business at its visitor center north of Buhl on the Snake River. Little kids in particular love to press their noses against the underground fish-viewing window, where trout swim by within inches and huge sturgeon can be seen dwelling in the murkier depths. The center has good picnicking grounds, too.

In Buhl itself, *Cloverleaf Creamery* at 205 South Broadway is the retail face of a family-run operation that uses old-fashioned techniques to coax and bottle milk from its small herd a few miles down the road. Stop by for an

Sage, Wind, and Stone

A few weeks after our daughter, Natalie, was born in 1994, Bruce and I took a Sunday afternoon drive to the Snake River between Hagerman and Bliss. We'd come to watch kayakers negotiate a new stretch of rapids created by a rock slide a year or so before.

We parked our car and walked the narrow dirt path down to the river, our child cradled in a baby carrier against my chest. Along the way, I picked a sprig of sagebrush and held it to Natalie's nose. Her tiny nostrils flared at the sweet, pungent scent. "This is what Idaho smells like," I told her.

At that moment, I realized my own Idaho walks have given me an intimate knowledge of the place where I live—things I would never know if I never left my car. What freshly picked sage smells like, for example, and how south winds blow much warmer than west winds, and how lava rock ranges from smooth and sinewy to rough and jagged. I adopted this state, and so I came to this understanding as an adult. For my little native Idahoan, however, these facts were the fabric of her childhood. No matter where she may live, Natalie will have immutable memories of sage, of wind, and of stone.

ice-cream cone, or call (208) 543-4272 ahead of time to ask about touring the nearby dairy where every cow has a name.

The *Eighth Street Center for Peace* is one of Buhl's most beautiful landmarks, a former church that is now an interfaith sanctuary and home to a variety of classes, concerts, art exhibits, and private parties. An outdoor labyrinth is available for strolling year-round. For more information call (208) 543-5417 or see eighthstreetcenter.com.

A short drive southwest of Buhl leads to *Balanced Rock,* a curious geological formation that appears poised like a giant mushroom (or maybe a question mark?) against the blue Idaho sky. The landmark is just a few miles west of Castleford, and a nearby small county park along Salmon Falls Creek provides another perfect spot for a picnic, fishing, and tent camping. To get there follow the signs out of Buhl for 16 miles.

Clover, a small farming community due east of Castleford, is the setting for one of Idaho's most beautiful country churches, built in 1918. *Clover Lutheran Church* has long served the families of the area, and the parishioners have given back to the church in equal measure, most notably through the stained-glass windows that grace the north and south sides of the sanctuary. These windows, done in traditional leaded stained-glass style, were made entirely by members of the congregation. The windows on the south side depict the local farming community, including sprigs of clover; those on the north are rich in Christian symbolism. The church also has its original ceiling of embossed tin.

Sunday morning would be the best time to see Clover Lutheran, hear its pipe organ, and visit with the congregation. Services are at 9:30 a.m. But the church is worth a stop at any time. If no one's in the office on the building's northwest side, check at the parsonage, located at the ranch house just to the north. The church cemetery also is notable for its headstones, some of which are in the native German of the people who settled Clover. The oldest graves are in the cemetery's southwest corner.

Just east of Filer, US 93 swings south from US 30 for the Nevada border some 40 miles away. Just over the Nevada line, *Jackpot* serves as the gambling hub for Idaho (and, judging from license plates in the casino parking lots, for revelers from as far away as Montana, Manitoba, and Saskatchewan, too). The town's biggest draw is *Cactus Pete's,* a full-fledged resort with comfortable rooms, abundant dining options (including an excellent buffet and upscale steak-and-seafood house), major musical acts in an outdoor amphitheater, and semi-big-name entertainment in the casino showroom. But some folks prefer the down-home, distinctly non-Vegas atmosphere of the town's smaller casinos, especially *Barton's Club 93.*

US 93 is also the best jumping-off spot for the Jarbidge country, one of the West's most wild and remote areas, located about 60 miles southwest of Rogerson. (All but the last 17 miles are paved.) Although on the Nevada border like Jackpot, Jarbidge's main attraction isn't gambling but natural splendor: The *Jarbidge Mountains* boast eight peaks higher than 10,000 feet (the highest concentration in Nevada), and campers, hikers, and horseback riders will swear they've found paradise. Casual visitors will find primitive campsites along the Jarbidge River or indoor accommodations at the Outdoor Inn, which also serves food. For people eager to explore the wilderness, Lowell Prunty's *Jarbidge Wilderness Guide & Packing* offers horse packing, backpacking, and hunting trips. For more information call (208) 857-2270 or see jarbidgeadventures.com. Have a look at *Nevada Off the Beaten Path* for more ideas on seeing the Silver State.

If you're heading into Twin Falls from the west via US 30, stop a few miles west of town to check out the *Twin Falls County Historical Museum* in the old Union School. From fancy old hats to agricultural equipment, the museum has a bit of everything that made life tick in early Twin Falls. Of special note is the display on pioneer-era photographer Clarence Bisbee, a colorful character who chronicled the city's growth for many decades. Displays rotate every other month, so there's always something new to see. The museum is located at 21337A US 30, just east of the Curry Crossing. Hours

The Filer Fair

Filer is home to the **Twin Falls County Fair and Magic Valley Stampede,** which the *Los Angeles Times* once named one of the top ten rural county fairs in the United States. The "Filer Fair," as it's known locally, runs the six days up to and including Labor Day. It's big enough to draw top-name country singers and rodeo cowboys, yet small enough to retain a real down-home feel. For many Southern Idahoans, the fair recalls a reunion, high time to get caught up on gossip and marvel at how much the kids have grown.

The fair also provides a ready excuse to forget your diet for a while: For some of the most unusual fare, check the one-of-a-kind troutburgers served up by the Buhl Catholic Church, or the tater pigs—a link sausage stuffed inside an Idaho baked potato—offered by the Magichords, a local barbershop singing group. You'll also find everything from fried Oreos to hamburgers to homemade pies and gyros. Just remember to visit the carnival rides before you eat, not after! Get more info and this year's dates at tfcfair.com.

are noon to 5 p.m. Tues through Sat, Mar through Dec (or by appointment), and admission is free, although donations are welcome. Call (208) 736-4675 or visit twinfallsmuseum.org for more information. If the small Bisbee exhibit here piques your interest, you can see more of his work at the Twin Falls Public Library, where his photo collection is stored. (Some of it can also be viewed online at flickr.com/photos/twinfallspubliclibrary.)

The Magic Valley

At the heart of the Magic Valley is Twin Falls, the largest city in South Central Idaho, with a population of about 42,000. Few towns can match Twin Falls for an impressive "front door," in this case the majestic *Snake River Canyon.* The chasm was created by the Bonneville Flood, which came roaring from prehistoric Lake Bonneville through Southeastern Idaho's Red Rock Pass about 15,000 years ago. At its peak the flood spewed 15 million cubic feet of water per second, or three times the flow of the Amazon River, carving the massive canyon that now serves as a welcome mat to Twin Falls.

The gorge is spanned by the *Perrine Bridge,* a 1,500-foot-long engineering marvel standing 486 feet above the river. When the first Perrine Bridge was completed in 1927, it was the highest cantilever bridge for its length in the world. The present span was completed in 1976, and visitors can view the canyon from overlooks on either rim or from a walkway on the bridge itself. Don't worry if you see people leaping from the bridge. They are BASE jumpers (BASE stands for bridge, antenna, span, and earth), and Twin Falls is one of the most popular places in the world for enthusiasts of this extreme sport because the Perrine Bridge is one of the only spots in the world where it's legal to jump year-round. Bear in mind, however, that BASE jumping is only for experienced sky divers who have the proper equipment and training.

Twin Falls recently renovated its visitor center, with floor-to-ceiling window views of the Perrine Bridge and canyon. Displays tell the story of the area's unusual irrigation-based agricultural history, and helpful volunteers can offer advice on other local attractions and activities.

Of course, the canyon itself is a major draw, and not just for daredevils. Head down Canyon Springs Road—ask for directions at the visitor center or watch for the signs—to drive into its depths. After a few twists and turns, you'll see *Centennial Waterfront Park,* which has good picnicking, boat launches, and canoe, kayak, and stand-up paddleboard rentals from A Way of Life Adventure Sports. See prices and details at paddlethesnake.com. *Canyon Springs Golf Course* is open to the public and a bargain at about $35 for eighteen holes on summer weekends, especially given the scenery. Fees are lower fall through spring and on summer weekdays. See more and book a tee time at canyonspringsgolf.com. Continue on past the golf course until the road ends, and you'll be at the trailhead for *Auger Falls,* a lightly developed city park where several miles of hiking and mountain biking trails afford access to 500 acres along the Snake River.

There are trails on the canyon rim, too, along with some culture. The Twin Falls Center for the Arts at 195 River Vista Place includes the *Full Moon Gallery.* This artists' co-op showcases locally created fine artworks and contemporary craft items. Browse for paintings, pottery, photography, jewelry, and more. Hours are 10 a.m. to 5 p.m. Tues through Fri. For more information call (208) 734-2787 or visit magicvalleyartscouncil.org.

You might think there'd be restaurants lining the canyon rim, but there are only a few. In the same building as the arts council, *Elevation 486* is open daily for lunch and dinner, with outdoor tables and twice-daily happy hours (from 3 to 6 p.m. and again from 9 p.m. to closing). *Canyon Crest Dining & Event Center* at 330 Canyon Crest Dr. is more oriented toward private parties, but it also has lunch and dinner daily, plus Sunday brunch and monthly wine dinners. Get to this area via the hiking-biking rim trails from the city visitor center by the Perrine Bridge, or drive Pole Line Road west past Costco, then turn north (right) on Washington Street.

To reach the heart of Twin Falls, take Blue Lakes Boulevard south from the canyon, then a half-right onto Shoshone Street at the intersection with US 30 (Addison Avenue). *City Park* is home to open-air concerts by a municipal band every Thurs night June through early Aug. A few blocks away along Main

Avenue, a new downtown plaza includes a splash-pad play area and areas for concerts and festivals. ***Twin Beans Coffee*** at 144 Main Ave. East has a front-row seat to the new amenities, along with coffee drinks from beans roasted on-site and sandwiches, salads, and crepes with names that'll please the most ardent geek pop-culture fan. (Think *Harry Potter, Sherlock, Dr. Who,* and even *Firefly.*) Down the street, ***O'Dunken's Draught House,*** a friendly, well-lit tavern at the intersection of Main Avenue and Shoshone Street, is the local version of Cheers, but with a decidedly Idaho flavor. O'Dunken's offers an excellent selection of beers and ales from the Northwest and beyond, and the walls—a veritable capsule history of Twin Falls—are a sight to see.

Travelers who are as interested in preparing food as they are in eating it will enjoy a stop at ***Rudy's—A Cook's Paradise*** at 147 Main Ave. West. From Dutch-oven gear to gourmet kitchenware to regional specialty foods, you'll find it here. There's also a good selection of fine wine and beer, as well as regular cooking classes taught by some of the region's most acclaimed chefs. On the first Fri of many months, look for live music and libations from 6 to 9 p.m. Regular hours are 9 a.m. to 6 p.m. Mon through Fri and 9 a.m. to 5:30 p.m. Sat. Call (208) 733-5477 or see cooksparadise.com for more information on upcoming classes and events.

One of Twin Falls' best assets is the ***College of Southern Idaho,*** with a pretty 300-acre campus that has lots of trees and walking trails. CSI's ***Herrett Center for Arts and Science*** includes an anthropology museum of pre-Columbian artifacts; a contemporary, regional art gallery; Idaho's largest planetarium theater; and a public observatory. The 24-inch research-grade telescope is among the largest wheelchair-accessible telescopes in the world. Free and low-cost public viewing events are scheduled regularly. The Herrett's jungle archaeology exhibit features iguanas, snakes, lizards, and frogs within a simulated scientific field research station from the Central American rain forest. The Herrett Center is open Tues through Sat. Call (208) 732 6655 or visit csi.edu/ herrett to see current hours and planetarium showtimes.

A few miles east of Twin Falls, ***Shoshone Falls*** ranks among Idaho's most impressive sights. Sometimes called the Niagara of the West, this cataract is actually 212 feet tall, or nearly 40 feet higher than Niagara Falls. The main overlook is a good one, but if you'd like a less-seen vista, head up the steep trail on the opposite end of the viewpoint parking lot. Up the hill the trail meets a road (now closed to traffic) that becomes a path to several other viewpoints where you might be able to enjoy the falls in solitude.

Shoshone Falls is best seen in springtime before much of the Snake River's runoff is diverted for agricultural irrigation. (See a webcam showing current water flows on the Shoshone Falls page at tfid.org.) But even when the flow

Avenging Evel Knievel

When Evel Knievel tried to jump a rocket-powered motorcycle across the Snake River Canyon on September 8, 1974, tens of thousands of people watched in person; future screenwriter Joe Eszterhas wrote a novella-length cover story on the event for *Rolling Stone*; and the Ideal Toy Company claimed to have sold more than $125 million worth of Knievel toys. Knievel put Twin Falls on the map in a big way, even though the actual stunt proved a dud when the daredevil's parachute malfunctioned and he and his cycle plunged into the river.

On September 16, 2016, when Hollywood stuntman Eddie Braun actually did jump the canyon a few miles east of where Knievel tried, the event drew much less notice. Onlookers numbered in the hundreds, and Braun put more than a million dollars of his own money into the project when corporations balked at his sponsorship bids. Still, for Braun, the jump seemed less about fame and more about honoring his boyhood hero's memory and proving that Knievel could have made it. (The audience reportedly included Robbie Knievel, who several times unsuccessfully sought permission from Idaho officials to avenge his father's most spectacular failure. It also was a great day for engineer Scott Truax, whose dad Robert designed Knievel's Sky-Cycle X-2 in 1974.)

Knievel's Great Snake River Canyon Jump went awry, but memories of the attempt still loom large in South Central Idaho, even after Braun's successful leap. That's why many visitors to Twin Falls gape upriver from the Perrine Bridge at the dirt remains of **Evel Knievel's launch site** on the south rim, and why boaters sometimes scan the canyon's north wall for Knievel's supposed "target," still visible just below the rim. To see the section of canyon that Braun cleared, head to the Hansen Bridge, just south of exit 182 on I-84, and look east. Braun flew on a steam-powered rocket from the north rim of the canyon to a farmer's field on the south side.

slows, the falls and adjacent Dierkes Lake Park are well worth visitors' attention any time of year. Swimming, fishing, rock climbing, picnicking, and boating are among the available activities, and an easy hike back to Dierkes's "Hidden Lakes" is pleasant (at least if you overlook the behemoth homes rising above the canyon wall). If you ever happen to be here on New Year's Day, be sure to stop by the impoundment above Shoshone Falls to watch intrepid water skiers raise funds for local charities in the "Freeze on Skis" event.

South Central Idaho is Oregon Trail country, and one trading post used by the emigrants—the ***Rock Creek Stage Station***—can still be seen 5 miles south of Hansen. (Follow the signs off US 30 east of Twin Falls.) Built in 1865 by James Bascom, the log store at the site is the oldest building in South Central Idaho. Interpretive signs tell how the site (also called Stricker Ranch, after a later owner) served the pioneers at the intersection of the Oregon Trail, Ben Holladay's Overland Stage route, and the Kelton Road from Utah. The old

Stricker House, also on the grounds, is open Sun afternoons Apr through Sept. Shaded picnic facilities are available. Call (208) 423-4000 for more information.

The road south from Hansen continues along Rock Creek into the Twin Falls district of the Sawtooth National Forest, known locally as the **South Hills.** Long considered a private playground by Twin Falls–area residents, the South Hills offer good trails for hiking, horseback riding, cross-country skiing, mountain biking, all-terrain vehicle sports, and snowmobiling. Facilities include several campgrounds and picnic areas, along with the small, family-run **Magic Mountain Ski Area,** where full-day lift tickets run $31 for adults and $22 for children and teens. There's a tubing hill, too. Get more info at magicmountainresort.com. The Pike Mountain overlook not far past the ski resort makes a fitting turnaround for anyone on a scenic drive. Call the Forest Service office at (208) 737-3200 for more information.

During World War II more than 110,000 American citizens of Japanese descent were rounded up from the West Coast and incarcerated farther inland. Many from the Seattle area were transported to the Minidoka War Relocation Center, or **Hunt Camp,** as it came to be known. At one time nearly 10,000 people lived at Hunt, making it Idaho's eighth-largest city. Conditions in the camp were less than ideal. People lived in cramped tar-paper shacks. Guards were posted and prisoners told they would be shot if they moved too close to the barbed-wire fences. Despite the hardship and indignities, about one in ten camp residents wound up serving in the US Armed Forces during World War II.

Little remains of the camp, but it is being protected by the National Park Service as the **Minidoka National Historic Site.** A short trail identifies

Snake River Thrills

When most people think about Snake River floats, they picture raft trips in the shadows of the Grand Tetons in Wyoming. But the Snake River near Twin Falls is becoming the destination of choice for many serious white-water junkies. In years of heavy snowfall, the resulting spring runoff turns the Snake's 14-mile Murtaugh Section (just downstream from Caldron Linn) into a thrill fest for expert kayakers, and several other nearby stretches are nearly as challenging.

These advanced-level river runs shouldn't be taken lightly. Inquire locally on conditions and precautions before you set out. Better yet, get on a guided trip. Area chambers of commerce and sporting goods stores can recommend a good outfitter; Olin and Shelley Gardner of Idaho Guide Service at (208) 734-4998 are among the most experienced in these waters, and they also run canoe trips to the base of Shoshone Falls when water levels allow it. Have a look at idahoguideservice.com for more information and pictures of what you can expect.

historic structures including the waiting room and guard station, both made of lava, and exhibits pay tribute to residents who died in the war. Of particular note are the half-dozen or so baseball diamonds—the prisoners found some solace and entertainment in pickup ball games—and the fields where evacuees grew various crops for the war effort. The site is located a little more than 2 miles north of Highway 25, 7 miles west of Eden. A pair of Idaho highway historical signs—one on Hunt, the other on Prehistoric Man—marks the turn.

The Prehistoric Man sign refers to nearby **Wilson Butte Cave,** an archaeological site of great importance. Artifacts from Wilson Butte Cave near Eden have been carbon dated at 14,500 years old, making them among the oldest findings in the New World. There are no interpretive displays at the cave, but it can be found by driving 2 miles north of the Hunt Camp, then 3.7 miles west. Here the road turns to dirt and, in 2 more miles, crosses a canal. A sign another half-mile or so down the road points the way to the cave, still 2 miles away.

Shoshone Falls gets all the publicity, but **Caldron Linn**—or Star Falls, as it's sometimes called—merits its own mighty place in the Snake River Hall of Fame. It was here the 1811 Wilson Price Hunt fur-trapping expedition gave up the river after losing one of its most valuable members, Canadian boatman Antoine Clappine, in the rapids nearby. A year later, according to Cort Conley's *Idaho for the Curious*, Robert Stuart returned to the scene and made this journal entry: "In one place at the Caldron Linn the whole body of the river is confined between two ledges of rock somewhat less than 40 feet apart and here indeed its terrific appearance beggars all description—Hecate's caldron was never half so agitated when vomiting even the most diabolical spells, as is this Linn in a low stage of water."

Caldron Linn can be reached from I-84 by taking Valley Road south of exit 188. After about 3 miles, the road swings east and hits Murtaugh Road a mile east. Follow Murtaugh Road to the canyon and watch for the signs. If you cross the Murtaugh Bridge over the Snake River, you've gone too far. Also keep an eye on kids and pets near Caldron Linn. It's still a nasty, turbulent piece of river real estate.

Lava is the dominant feature of the landscape north of the Snake River Canyon. North and east of Shoshone, the Lincoln County seat, the roadways are rimmed with rugged lava flows that rolled over the land between 2,000 and 15,000 years ago. Some are **lava tubes,** created when a shell formed around a still-flowing river of lava. When the lava moved on, the shell remained. Some of these lava tubes may be explored; the Shoshone office of the Bureau of Land Management at (208) 732-7200 can provide information on locations and necessary equipment.

For another fascinating look at the area's geology, stop by the ***Black Magic Canyon*** wayside exhibit just south of the Lincoln-Blaine county line at the junction of Highway 75 and West Magic Road. This small but impressive canyon, full of potholes and weirdly sculpted boulders, was carved when pebbles and cobbles from nearby mountain ranges were swept along by melting glacial waters from the last ice age. The best time to explore the canyon is late fall or winter; stay out if there's water in the channel.

Shoshone had Southern Idaho's last passenger railroad depot before Amtrak ended the Pioneer service that used to come through between Salt Lake City and Boise. Despite unsuccessful efforts to revive the line, Shoshone retains its rail-town feel, and it's also seen a bit of a building boom in recent decades as people get priced out of Sun Valley 60 miles to the north. (With light traffic and a good supply of music or audiobooks, locals have no problem making distant commutes over the desert.) If you're just passing through, get a bite at the ***Manhattan Cafe*** at 133 South Rail St. West. One of Idaho's oldest restaurants, dating to the late 1800s, it has a basic but extensive menu, daily specials, and plenty of small-town character.

Mini-Cassia Land

A high-desert oasis not far from the freeway, ***Lake Walcott State Park,*** northeast of Rupert via Highway 24, is along the portion of the Snake River stopped short by Minidoka Dam. The park is located within the Minidoka National Wildlife Refuge, where migratory waterfowl including ducks, geese, and tundra swans rest on their fall and spring journeys. Lake Walcott caters to campers, horseback riders, picnickers, and growing ranks of windsurfers. There's also an eighteen-hole flying disc golf course, so bring your Frisbees. For more information see parksandrecreation.idaho.gov/parks/lake-walcott.

Minidoka Dam itself also is worth a look. Built starting in 1904 the dam became the first federal hydroelectric power project in the Northwest. Along with Milner Dam near Murtaugh, Minidoka Dam made possible the irrigation and settlement of southern Idaho's fertile but dry soil. Recreation access was improved when the dam's spillway and headworks were replaced between 2011 and 2015.

Rupert, the Minidoka County seat, has a charming town square that's listed on the National Register of Historic Places. In 1987 then-governor Cecil Andrus proclaimed that Rupert is ***Christmas City USA,*** at least in Idaho. Each year on the day after Thanksgiving, Rupert celebrates with Santa's arrival, holiday lighting, fireworks, and a chili feed. The town has a big Independence Day celebration every summer, too, with festivities starting several days before July 4. The **Minidoka County Historical Society Museum,** 99 East Baseline Rd., is open 10 a.m. to 3 p.m. Mon through Sat except holidays year-round, with admission by donation. Call (208) 436-0336 if you need more information.

Burley is best known for the **Idaho Regatta,** a major powerboating event held annually in late June; see idahoregatta.org for dates and information. Also in Burley, **Cassia County Historical Museum** at 1142 Hiland Ave. has exhibits telling of Idaho's farming, ranching, mining, and logging history. The museum is open 10 a.m. to 5 p.m. Tues through Sat, Apr through Sept.

Burley's main drag, Overland Avenue, turns into Highway 27, which heads south on a loop drive that takes the traveler back in time to one of the West's best-preserved Victorian towns, mountain scenery, and a world-class rock-climbing area. Seventeen miles south of Burley, the community of **Oakley** was settled around 1878 by Mormon pioneers and is famous for its impressive collection of fine historic buildings. Particularly notable landmarks include the Marcus Funk residence (on Center Avenue between Poplar and Main), the Oakley Co-op (at Main and Center), and Howells Castle (at Blaine and Poplar). Benjamin Howells, an early settler and judge, also built **Howells Opera House,** where the Oakley Valley Arts Council continues to present musical performances several times each year. Call (208) 677-ARTS or see oakleyvalleyartscouncil.org for information.

A self-guided tour of Oakley's notable homes is held every year on the third Sat in June. Call the city at (208) 362-3313 for information. You can even stay in one: the **Haight Home Bed & Breakfast** at 215 East Poplar St. dates to the 1890s and has rooms priced from $90 to $150. Check haighthomebed andbreakfast.com or call (208) 862-7829 for information.

The peaks rising to Oakley's east are the Albion Mountains, the loftiest in South Central Idaho. Inquire locally or call the Sawtooth National Forest's Burley Ranger District at (208) 678-0430 for directions into the high country. Day hikers and backpackers alike will enjoy a trek to **Independence Lakes,** four tiny blue gems tucked against 10,339-foot Cache Peak. **Lake Cleveland,** another locally popular outdoor playground atop adjacent Mount Harrison, may be accessed by motor vehicle. Camping, picnicking, and fishing are favorite pastimes here. **Pomerelle,** a family-friendly ski area featuring about two dozen runs and the region's only nighttime skiing, also is located on Mount Harrison. Pomerelle runs its chairlift in summertime, too, for scenic views and access to mountain biking and hiking trails. See pomerelle.com or call (208) 673-5555 for recorded information, including the ski report.

Southeast of Oakley, Emery Canyon Road provides access to the **City of Rocks National Reserve.** This 14,300-acre area was named by California

"Diamondfield" Jack Davis

Of all the characters in South Central Idaho lore, "Diamondfield" Jack Davis has had an unusually tenacious hold on the region's imagination for his role in the sheepmen vs. cattle owner wars of the 1890s. Hired by cattle magnate John Sparks to keep the rangeland near Oakley free from sheep, Davis earned a reputation as a scrappy fighter—so he was naturally fingered as the prime suspect when two sheepmen were found dead.

The 1897 Davis trial in Albion, then the Cassia County seat, might have been an ordinary one had it not been for the cast of supporting players. Davis's boss, John Sparks, hired James Hawley—the veteran of more than 300 murder cases and a future Idaho governor—to defend his watchman. The prosecution was mounted by William Borah, a young Boise lawyer who went on to become one of Idaho's most famous US senators. The jury swiftly found Davis guilty and sentenced him to hang.

A year later, area ranchers Jim Bower and Jeff Gray confessed to the killings—yet Davis remained on death row, a requested pardon denied.

Other legal maneuverings ensued, with papers filed all the way up to the US Supreme Court. Bower and Gray, tried for the murders, were acquitted on grounds of self-defense. Hawley sought a new trial for Davis, but his motion was denied—and Davis once again was ordered to the gallows. Many stays of execution later, Davis—by then jailed at the Idaho Penitentiary in Boise—was finally pardoned and set free in 1902. His first act on leaving the pen in Boise was stopping for a drink with the city's new mayor, Jim Hawley. Davis moved to Nevada, where he became a successful miner, only to squander his wealth and die in 1949 after being hit by a Las Vegas taxicab.

Trail pioneers passing through in the mid-nineteenth century, some of whom marked their names in axle grease on the ancient granite formations. "During the afternoon, we passed through a stone village composed of huge, isolated rocks of various and singular shapes, some resembling cottages, others steeples and domes," wrote Margaret Frink, who visited in 1850. "It is called City of Rocks, but I think the name Pyramid City [is] more suitable. It is a sublime, strange, and wonderful scene—one of nature's most interesting works." The City of Rocks' hoodoos, arches, caves, and monoliths are the result of erosion, not earthquakes or volcanic activity as some visitors suppose. Most of the rock is part of the Almo Pluton formation, about 25 million years old, while some is part of the 2.5-billion-year-old Green Creek Complex, among the oldest rock in the continental United States. Both kinds can easily be seen at the Twin Sisters formation. The darker "twin" is the older rock, the lighter is from the younger formation.

Today, City of Rocks is an irresistible lure to the legions of rock climbers who come here to scale the reserve's challenging spires, some sixty to seventy stories high. In addition to climbers and history buffs, the reserve beckons stargazers (who value the pitch-black sky), campers, mountain bikers, cross-country skiers, and sightseers. For more information call (208) 824-5901, see nps.gov/ciro, or stop by the reserve office in Almo. Nearby *Castle Rocks State Park* offers more rock-climbing terrain and good wildlife watching, plus a remodeled century-old ranch house that can sleep a big family and a separate bunkhouse also available for nightly rentals. See details at parksandrecreation .idaho.gov/parks/castle-rocks.

In Almo, look for *Durfee Hot Springs,* which has a 15-by-30-foot natural hot tub, a 50-by-50 swimming pool, a self-contained kiddie pool, and a gift shop showcasing works by local artists and crafters. The hot springs are at 2798 Elba-Almo Rd., and as its website at durfeehotsprings.com says, "days and hours change with the seasons, so it is best to call ahead for information." The number is (208) 824-5701. While you're in the area, be sure to have a meal at the *Almo Creek Outpost,* 3020 South Elba-Almo Rd. The steaks are huge, the beer is cold, and your dinner may be accompanied by some live old-time music.

For an extended stay in the area, consider the wagon and horseback trips led by Ken Jafek of *War Eagle Outfitters and Guides* in nearby Malta. Jafek's trips travel from Massacre Rocks to City of Rocks along the Raft River Valley, crossing the California Trail in several locations. He also offers hunting, fishing, and camping trips. For information call (208) 645-2455.

From Almo, the Cassia County loop and Highway 77 resume at the crossroads town of Connor. Head north 11 miles to Albion, notable as the former home of the *Albion State Normal School,* one of Idaho's leading teacher-training colleges. The school's beautiful campus is now home to several hospitality businesses. One is the *Albion Bed & Breakfast,* where you can stay in a remodeled classroom or rent the whole place for a family reunion or other gathering of up to forty-four people. Owner Chad Manderscheid, who has been doing most of the restoration himself, also runs the on-site Albion Schoolhouse Bakery. See albionbedandbreakfast.com for details and photos. The phone number is (208) 673-6474.

Another area business, *Albion Campus Retreat,* has renovated the former men's dorm, Miller Hall, and the college president's cottage as overnight accommodations. They're mostly for groups and retreats of up to seventy-five people, but check the rates page at albioncampusretreat.com or call (208) 312-8484 for nightly availability. *Haunted Mansions of Albion* tours run here on weekends each Halloween season, too.

Places to Stay in South Central Idaho

GOODING

Cottage Inn
1331 South Main St.
(208) 934-4055
motelingoodingid.com
Inexpensive

Gooding Hotel Bed & Breakfast
112 Main St.
(208) 934-4374
goodinghotelbandb.com
Moderate

WENDELL

Hub City Inn
115 South Idaho St.
(208) 536-2326
Inexpensive

HAGERMAN

Billingsley Creek Lodge
17940 US 30
(208) 837-4822
billingsleycreek.com
Inexpensive–Moderate

Hagerman Valley Inn
State and Hagerman
Streets
(208) 837-6196
hagermanvalleyinn.com
Inexpensive–Moderate

BUHL

Oregon Trail Motel
510 Broadway Ave. South
(US 30)
(208) 534-8814
oregontrailinn.com
Inexpensive

TWIN FALLS

Best Western Twin Falls Hotel
1377 Blue Lakes Blvd.
North
(208) 736-8000
bestwesternidaho.com
Moderate–Expensive

Blue Lakes Inn
952 Blue Lakes Blvd.
North
(208) 933-2123
bluelakesinn.com
Moderate–Expensive

The Fillmore Inn
102 Fillmore St.
(208) 736-4257
thefillmoreinn.com
Expensive

Hampton Inn
1658 Fillmore St. North
(208) 734-2233
hamptoninn.com
Moderate

La Quinta Inn & Suites
539 Pole Line Rd.
(208) 736-9600
lq.com
Moderate–Expensive

Quality Inn & Suites
1910 Fillmore Ave. North
(208) 734-7494
choicehotels.com
Moderate

Red Lion Hotel Canyon Springs
1357 Blue Lakes Blvd.
North
(208) 734-5000
redlion.com/twin-falls
Moderate–Expensive

JEROME

Best Western Sawtooth Inn & Suites
2653 South Lincoln St.
(208) 324-9200
bestwesternidaho.com
Moderate

Days Inn
I-84 exit 173
(208) 324-6400
daysinn.com
Inexpensive

BURLEY

Best Western Plus Burley Inn
800 North Overland Ave.
(208) 678-3501
bestwesternidaho.com
Moderate

Budget Motel
900 North Overland Ave.
(208) 678-2200
burleybudgetmotel.com
Inexpensive

Fairfield Inn & Suites
230 West Seventh St.
(208) 677-5000
marriott.com
Moderate

Super 8 Motel
336 South 600 West
(208) 678-7000
super8.com
Moderate

OAKLEY

Haight Home Bed & Breakfast
215 East Poplar St.
(208) 862-7829
haighthomebedand
breakfast.com
Moderate

HELPFUL WEBSITES FOR SOUTH CENTRAL IDAHO

Hagerman Fossil Beds National Monument
nps.gov/hafo

Hagerman visitor information
hagermanvalleychambercom

Southern Idaho Tourism
visitsouthidaho.com

Twin Falls Area Chamber of Commerce
twinfallschamber.com

The *Times-News* (Twin Falls newspaper)
magicvalley.com

City of Rocks National Reserve
nps.gov/ciro

Mini-Cassia Chamber of Commerce
minicassiachamber.com

ALMO

Old Homestead Bed & Breakfast
(Closed in winter)
809 East 2975 South
(208) 824-5521
Inexpensive

ALBION

Albion Bed & Breakfast
424 West Market St.
(208) 673-6474
albionbedandbreakfast.com
Moderate–Expensive

Marsh Creek Inn
on Highway 77
(208) 673-6259
Inexpensive–Moderate

Places to Eat in South Central Idaho

BLISS

Oxbow Cafe
(American)
199 East US 30
(208) 352-4250
Inexpensive

WENDELL

Farmhouse Restaurant
(American)
I-84 exit 157
(208) 536-6688
Inexpensive–Moderate

HAGERMAN

The Riverboat Restaurant
(American)
171 South State St.
(208) 837-4333
Inexpensive

Snake River Grill
(eclectic)
State and Hagerman Streets
(208) 837-6227
Inexpensive–Moderate

BUHL

Arctic Circle
(fast food)
606 Broadway Ave. South
(208) 543-5321
Inexpensive

La Plaza
(Mexican)
1206 Main St.
(208) 543-8600
Inexpensive

TWIN FALLS

Burger Stop
(American)
1335 Addison Ave. East
(208) 734-0427
Inexpensive

Canyon Crest
(fine dining)
330 Canyon Crest Dr.
(208) 733-9392
Moderate–Expensive

Elevation 486
(New American)
195 River Vista Place
(208) 737-0486
Moderate–Expensive

Emma's Cafe
(Bosnian)
669 Blue Lakes Blvd.
(208) 308-7007
Inexpensive

Gertie's Brick Oven Cookery
(pizza)
602 Second Ave. South
(208) 736-9110
Inexpensive

La Casita
(Mexican)
111 South Park Ave. West
(208) 734-7974
Inexpensive

Rock Creek
(steak/seafood)
200 Addison Ave. West
(208) 734-4154
Moderate–Expensive

Twin Beans Coffee
(American)
144 Main Ave. East
(208) 749-0927
Inexpensive

JEROME

Choate's Family Diner
(American)
400 West Main St.
(208) 324-4642
Inexpensive

La Campesina
(Mexican)
1323 South Lincoln Ave.
(208) 324-5438
Inexpensive–Moderate

SHOSHONE

Manhattan Cafe
(American)
133 South Rail St.
(208) 886-2142
Inexpensive

EDEN

Traveler's Oasis Restaurant
(American)
I-84 exit 182
(208) 825-4147
Inexpensive–Moderate

RUPERT

Connor's Cafe
(American)
I-84 exit 208
(208) 670-9007
Inexpensive

Henry's Drift Inn
(American)
545 F St.
(208) 436-1300
Moderate

HEYBURN

Stevo's
(American)
290 South 600 West
(208) 679-3887
Inexpensive–Moderate

BURLEY

Duck Ugly's
(American)
163 West US 30
(208) 878-3825
Inexpensive

Guadalajara Mexican Restaurant
262 Overland Ave.
(208) 678-8695
Inexpensive

ALMO

Almo Creek Outpost
(American)
3020 Elba-Almo Rd.
(208) 824-5577
Moderate–Expensive

ALSO WORTH SEEING IN SOUTH CENTRAL IDAHO

Snyder Winery
Buhl

Anderson Camp (pool, miniature golf)
Eden

Magic Valley Speedway
south of Twin Falls

Nat–Soo–Pah Hot Springs
Hollister

Shoshone Ice Caves
north of Shoshone

Southeastern Idaho

Southeastern Idaho serves as a microcosm of the history of American westward expansion. It was here that pioneers had to decide whether to jump off onto the California Trail for the gold country. It was here many others came north from Utah, following their Mormon leaders' orders to farm the land and settle new towns. And it was here many pressed on toward Oregon, pausing briefly for supplies and rest before crossing the rugged Snake River Plain.

I-86 enters Southeastern Idaho from the west, making a lonely crossing of Power County and part of the Fort Hall Indian Reservation before reaching Pocatello, the region's major city. At Pocatello, I-15 heads north and south; 25 miles south of town, travelers can hop off on US 30 to make a loop around the region via US 89, Highways 34 or 36, and US 91. Drivers may want to extend their explorations of Southeastern Idaho into Utah, because the border between these two states is blurrier than most, as we shall see.

For Southeastern Idaho travel information, call (888) 201-1063 or see seidaho.org.

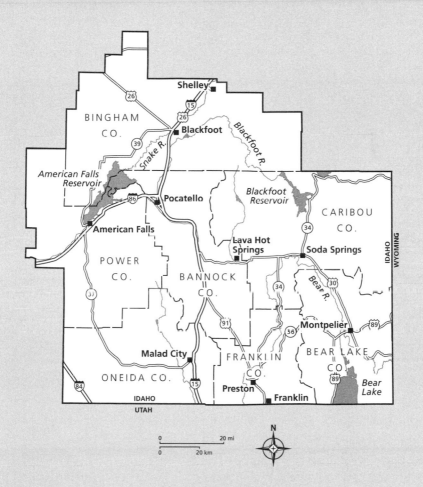

BINGHAM CO.

Shelley

Blackfoot

Snake R.

Blackfoot R.

American Falls Reservoir

Blackfoot Reservoir

Pocatello

CARIBOU CO.

American Falls

Lava Hot Springs

Soda Springs

POWER CO.

BANNOCK CO.

Bear R.

IDAHO WYOMING

Montpelier

Malad City

FRANKLIN CO.

BEAR LAKE CO.

ONEIDA CO.

Preston

Franklin

Bear Lake

IDAHO
UTAH

0   20 mi
0   20 km

N

Trails and Rails

Crossing Power County it's easy to get the feeling you're alone. Most travelers veer off the interstate either east of Burley, where I-84 runs southeast to Utah, or at I-15 at Pocatello. It's not hard to imagine what it might have been like for the pioneer wagon trains crossing the same stretch 150 years ago.

Most of those emigrants traversed southern Idaho without trouble from the Native Americans. But as traffic along the trail increased, the native peoples grew ever more resentful of the whites invading their land. This may have caused an August 1862 incident that led to the deaths of ten westward-bound emigrants and an unknown number of Shoshones in two days of fighting amid the lava outcroppings along the Snake River. During the emigrant era, the area became known as the Gate of Death or Devil's Gate because of a narrow, rocky passage through which the wagons rolled (now gone as a result of blasting for the construction of I-86). But stories of the 1862 battles eventually led the locals to dub the area Massacre Rocks.

Massacre Rocks State Park, situated on a narrow strip of land between I-86 and the Snake River, has made the most of its location. Hikers can trace history or see more than 200 species of birds and 300 varieties of desert plants along nearly 7 miles of trails. The park also has notable geologic features, many the result of extensive volcanic activity, others created by the massive Bonneville Flood, the second-largest flood in world geologic history. But things are quieter today. In addition to hiking, fishing, boating, and searching out the local flora and fauna, visitors can spend a peaceful respite in the park's campground or enjoy a game of disc golf with some very interesting natural hazards. Those making a brief stop in the area can combine a hike with a stop in the visitor center. Exhibits include the diary of Jane A. Gould, who traveled from Iowa to California in 1862 along the Oregon Trail and was in the area at the time of the skirmish with the Shoshones. For more information on Massacre Rocks, call (208) 548-2672 or see parksandrecreation.idaho.gov/parks/massacre-rocks.

Register Rock, located a few miles west of Massacre Rocks, was a favorite campground along the Oregon Trail, and many visiting emigrants signed their names on a large basalt boulder that is now the centerpiece of a small park. Some signatures date from as early as 1849, and many are still legible. On a smaller rock nearby, J. J. Hansen, a seven-year-old emigrant boy, carved a Native American's head in 1866. Nearly five decades later, after he had become a professional sculptor, Hansen returned and dated the rock again. Register Rock's shady picnic area offers welcome relief from the searing Idaho summer.

For an interesting detour off the interstate between American Falls and Blackfoot, consider taking Highway 39. This 55-mile route (as opposed to 47

AUTHOR'S FAVORITES IN
SOUTHEASTERN IDAHO

Idaho Potato Museum
Blackfoot

Lava Hot Pools
Lava Hot Springs

Museum of Clean
Pocatello

Bear Lake
on the Idaho-Utah border

Harkness Hotel
McCammon

National Oregon/California Trail Center
Montpelier

miles via the interstate) offers a pleasant two-lane alternative through several small towns and a lot of pretty potato country on the north side of *American Falls Reservoir.* Watch for the signs showing access to fishing on the human-made lake.

South and east of the reservoir, many Native Americans from the Shoshone and Bannock tribes live on the 544,000-acre *Fort Hall Indian Reservation,* which stretches across much of Power, Bannock, and Bingham Counties. Fort Hall is the most populous of Idaho's four reservations, with about 3,200 people living within its boundaries.

The *Shoshone-Bannock Festival* is held the second week of each August, and the tribes also operate a bunch of tourist-oriented businesses including the *Fort Hall Casino* and *Shoshone-Bannock Hotel* at exit 80 off of I-15. The casino restaurant, the Buffalo Horn Grill, serves traditional tribal specialties such as bison burgers, Indian tacos, and fry bread. The hotel's Cedar Spa offers a range of treatments including several with a regional flair, like the Great Salt Lake detoxifying body wrap and basalt hot stone massage. Room rates start at about $90. Call (208) 238-4800 or see shobanhotel.com for info.

The Oregon Trail really did pass through what is now the Fort Hall Reservation—and there truly was a Fort Hall on what is now reservation land, too. Nathaniel Wyeth established the outpost near the banks of the Snake River in 1834, selling it to the British Hudson's Bay Company three years later. It was a busy place, teeming first with fur trappers and traders and later with emigrants through the mid-1850s. There is nothing left of the original Fort Hall, but there are wagon ruts, emigrant grave sites, and other traces of the fort's history scattered across what is now known as the *Fort Hall Bottoms.* A replica of the fort stands in Pocatello's Ross Park.

Blackfoot, located just north of the reservation, narrowly lost an 1880 bid to replace Boise as capital of the Idaho Territory. Instead the city has become the Potato Capital of Idaho and probably the world. Potatoes have long been synonymous with Idaho, and Blackfoot is the seat of and largest town in Bingham County, the state's top spud-producing region. Small wonder, then, that Blackfoot's top attraction is the *Idaho Potato Museum.* The world's largest potato chip—of the Pringles variety, 25 by 14 inches, the equivalent of eighty regular chips—is on display, as is a photo of Marilyn Monroe modeling an Idaho potato sack. Picnic grounds are available, but there's also the Potato Station Cafe that serves up fries, baked potatoes with toppings, and even ice cream that looks like a baked spud. The museum is located in downtown Blackfoot at 130 Northwest Main St. in the old train depot. Hours are 9:30 a.m. to 5 p.m. Mon through Sat Apr through Sept, and 9:30 a.m. to 3 p.m. weekdays Oct through Mar. Admission is $3 for adults, $2.50 for seniors over age 55 and AAA members, and $1 for children ages 6 through 12. For more information call (208) 785-2517 or see idahopotatomuseum.com.

North of Blackfoot on I-15, meanwhile, travelers will notice the vast lava beds to the west. *Hell's Half Acre Lava Field,* located midway between Blackfoot and Idaho Falls, is a 180-square-mile flow that has been designated a National Natural Landmark. This is a relatively young lava field, with the last eruptions probably taking place about 2,000 years ago (although the flows near the interstate are probably twice that old). Hikers have two options here: a short educational loop trail (marked by blue-topped poles) that takes about a half-hour to traverse, or a 4.5-mile route that leads to the vent, or source, of the lava flow. The way to the vent is marked by red-topped poles, and the hike takes a full day. Be sure to wear boots with sturdy soles and carry plenty of water.

Pocatello, a city of about 55,000 people, apparently took its name from that of Pocataro, a Shoshone chief, but it owes its prominence—and a lot of its character—to railroading. The Utah and Northern narrow-gauge and Oregon Short Line railways, both part of the Union Pacific system, intersected at Pocatello,

TOP ANNUAL EVENTS IN SOUTHEASTERN IDAHO

Portneuf Greenway RiverFest
Pocatello (Aug)

Idaho Spud Day
Shelley (mid-Sept)

Shoshone-Bannock Festival
Fort Hall (early Aug)

Dogapoolooza
Lava Hot Springs (Sept)

Eastern Idaho State Fair
Blackfoot (early Sept)

Idaho Festival of Lights
Preston (Thanksgiving through Christmas)

and railroad activity spurred settlement and construction. By World War II, more than 4,500 railroad cars passed through Pocatello each day. Sadly, there's no longer any passenger rail service from the grand old Union Pacific Depot on West Bonneville Street, but plenty of railroad retirees and train buffs live here. The **Pocatello Model Railroad and Historical Society** holds an open house from 10 a.m. to 2 p.m. the third Sat of every month in Building B-59 southwest of the Union Pacific depot, plus special holiday train exhibits during the same hours every Sat from Thanksgiving through the last Sat before Christmas.

Like all good-size American towns, Pocatello has its "on-the-beaten-path" commercial strips and its downtown soul—or as they call it here, "Old Town Pocatello." The **Old Town Pavilion** at 420 North Main St. is the scene of many community gatherings, including the Revive @ 5 summer concert series held each Wed late May through Labor Day from 5 to 8 p.m. The first Fri of each month is another good time to visit, with an art walk set from 5 to 8 p.m. The **Portneuf Valley Farmers Market** sets up downtown each Sat morning May through Oct, as well as Wed evenings late May through Aug.

Pocatello has some beautiful architecture in its central core. Stroll along **Garfield Avenue** 2 blocks west of Main Street to see some fine examples. The church at 309 North Garfield, shared by the local Congregationalists and Unitarian Universalists, dates back to 1904. The **Standrod House** at 648 North Garfield was built in 1901, its light gray and red sandstone quarried in nearby McCammon and hauled to the site by horse-drawn wagons. The city of Pocatello acquired and renovated the Standrod House in the 1970s, and for a time it regained its status as a community center and later a furniture store. It's now a private home, but it's worth walking by.

Across the Union Pacific tracks from the downtown core, a warehouse district offers several good places to eat, drink, and play. The **Bridge** at 815 South First Ave. is a classy, casually elegant spot open for lunch and dinner, while **Portneuf Valley Brewing** at 615 South First Ave. has been crafting beer since 1996 and pours its creations daily from 11 a.m. to 11 p.m. The brewery also has food, wine, live music, art shows, and plenty of attitude in its marketing. ("Beer like your mom used to make" was the message on one billboard south of town, and PVB's founder and brewer is indeed a woman, the marvelously named Penny Pink.) The **Westside Players** present several dinner theater shows each year at the Warehouse, 1009 South Second Ave. See upcoming productions at westsideplayers.org.

Pocatello is home to Idaho State University, which enrolls about 12,750 students. Notable campus attractions include the **Idaho Museum of Natural History** at Fifth Avenue and Dillon Street and the hilltop 123,000-square-foot **L. E. and Thelma E. Stephens Performing Arts Center,** which looks

Cleaning Up in Pocatello

Don Aslett spent most of his life building a cleaning empire, so it's fitting that he has also created a museum celebrating tidiness: the **Museum of Clean** at 711 South Second Ave. in Pocatello's warehouse district.

Aslett, a Twin Falls native, began a janitorial services company now known as Varsity Facility Services while still in college at Idaho State University. Later, he launched a chain of cleaning supply stores, wrote more than thirty books about cleaning topics, and made many TV appearances. He's a history buff, too, and when he landed a collection of 250 vintage vacuum cleaners, he decided to start a museum.

The Museum of Clean is a work in progress, but it's definitely worth a stop (and you'll probably wish you had more time than you expected you'd spend here; two hours would be about right). In addition to retro cleaning gear of all kinds, there are exhibits on everything from plants that clean the air to a comically overstuffed garage to an orchestra diorama featuring historic personalities playing musical instruments crafted from trash. Kids will have fun here, and grown-ups will learn plenty, too.

If Aslett himself doesn't serve as your personal guide, you may take the tour with his nephew, Brad Kisling, who is quick with the quips and also wrote much of the funny copy on the museum's exhibits. It's fine to wander around on your own, too. The Museum of Clean is open from 10 a.m. to 5 p.m. Tues through Sat. Admission is $6 for everyone age 12 and up, $5 for kids ages 3 to 11, or $20 for a family (two adults and three children). Call (208) 236-6906 or see museumofclean.com.

something like a cross between a Mormon temple and the Taj Mahal. For more information on activities and events at ISU, see isu.edu.

Near the city's southern edge, ***Ross Park*** has many attractions including the Fort Hall Replica, Zoo Idaho, and an aquatics complex with a waterslide and "lazy river" feature. The ***Bannock County Historical Museum,*** also located here, is a good place to learn more about Pocatello's railroading past; other exhibits include war memorabilia, Native American artifacts, a restored stagecoach, and rooms that offer glimpses into how early Pocatello lived and worked. The museum is open from 10 a.m. to 6 p.m. Mon through Sat and 1 to 5 p.m. Sun Memorial Day weekend through Labor Day and 10 a.m. to 4 p.m. Tues through Sat the rest of the year. Summer admission to the museum, Fort Hall Replica, and Pocatello Junction Village is $4 for adults, $3 for seniors and military, and $2 for kids ages 6 and up. It's $2 for adults and $1 for kids the rest of the year, when the fort and pioneer village are closed. The phone number is (208) 233-0434.

Twenty-five miles south of Pocatello, the town of McCammon owes much of its existence to the business smarts of Henry Harkness, who built an empire along the Portneuf River that included a toll bridge, a lumber mill, ranches, and a grand opera house. This entrepreneurial legacy lives on at the ***Harkness Hotel,*** built in 1906 as the McCammon State Bank. Owner Aaron Hunsaker grew up in McCammon, went away to college, and met his wife, Arianne, in Washington, D.C., before moving back to his hometown to create a boutique hotel with gorgeous, high-ceilinged suites that are among the sweetest in Idaho. Rates start at $109 for rooms that would cost twice as much in Boise and three or four times as much on the West Coast. Most would be perfect for a romantic retreat, though several are large enough for families, and all have distinct design touches. A spa opened in 2016, with plans for several more rooms and an eventual restaurant. Watch the progress at theharknesshotel.com, and book online or with a call to (208) 254-4340.

Hot Baths and Pioneer Paths

The entire state of Idaho is justly famous for its hot springs, but no town in the state has been so blessed with wondrous thermal activity as ***Lava Hot Springs,*** situated along US 30 and the Portneuf River 35 miles southeast of Pocatello.

Tucked in a mile-high mountain valley near the north edge of the Wasatch Range, Lava Hot Springs once served as a winter campground for the Bannock and Shoshone Indian tribes, who thought the local springs held healing powers. Geologists believe the springs have been a consistent 110°F for at least 50 million years. The springs are rich with minerals—calcium carbonate, sodium chloride, and magnesium carbonate being most prevalent—but have no sulfur and, therefore, none of the nose-wrinkling odor typical of many hot springs.

The town has two main attractions, both operated by the Lava Hot Springs Foundation, a State of Idaho agency. A huge free-form Olympic pool complex on the west side of town has one third of an acre of water surface, 50-meter racing lanes, a 10-meter diving tower, several waterslides, and a surrounding carpet of green grass for sunbathing; another indoor 25-yard pool nearby meets Amateur Athletic Union standards. The latest addition is Portneuf Kiddie Cove, an indoor water playground that opens up to the outdoor pools in summer. The Olympic pool is open mid-May through Labor Day, while the indoor facilities are open year-round.

The Lava Hot Pools on the east side of town are perfect for mellow soaking. These geothermal mineral water baths—open every day of the year except Thanksgiving and Christmas—are set amid the sunken gardens of an extinct volcano and range in temperature from 102° to 112°F. One fee ($16 on summer weekends; $12.50 Mon through Thurs in summer; discounts mid-Sep through May) buys all-day admission to both the pools and the hot baths; discounts are available for children and senior citizens. Family discounts are offered on

Wed except holidays. Swimsuits, towels, and lockers may be rented, and group rates are available. Call (800) 423-8597 or visit lavahotsprings.com for hours and more information.

The pools, hot baths, and Portneuf River tubing have made Lava Hot Springs justly popular, so there are more places to stay here than in many much larger towns. One of the most interesting spots in town is the **Lava Hot Springs Inn,** a European-style bed-and-breakfast complete with an on-site massage therapist and several outdoor natural mineral-water pools. (One is 80 feet long, with room for swimming. Another is a water therapy pool for aquatic bodywork.) Rooms in the inn and several adjacent properties start at about $95 for basic accommodations and go to $395 for a four-bedroom house. The inn supposedly has its own ghost, too. For more information call (208) 776-5830 or see lavahotspringsinn.com.

Lava, as the town is known to locals, has plenty of restaurants at all price levels. For a special meal, head to the **Portneuf Grille & Lounge** in the Riverside Hot Springs Inn at 255 East Portneuf St., which offers creative fine dining and wine pairings. Fans of Thai food will want to be sure to have a meal at the **Riverwalk Cafe,** 695 East Main St. This small, family-run restaurant in a converted gas station serves authentic, inexpensive fare every day but Mon. For picnic goods, **Miho's Market** at 30 Main St. has an extensive deli counter.

Lava is a fun place to visit in any season, but autumn may be the best time of all. The crowds thin out, room rates dip even lower, and the surrounding hills are ablaze with some of Idaho's most colorful fall foliage. For more information on Lava Hot Springs, call (208) 776-5500 or see lavahotsprings.org.

Back on US 30 heading east from Lava Hot Springs, consider one of three short side trips to Black Canyon, Maple Grove Hot Springs, or the ghost town of Chesterfield. **Black Canyon** is one of Idaho's hidden geological gems. The gorge gets its start just downstream of the town of Grace, which is located about 5 miles south of US 30 via Highway 34. Turn west on Center Street in town (Turner Road) and pause at the bridge to see the chasm opening up. As the Bear River rolls across the farmland surrounding Grace, it quickly widens and deepens into a canyon rivaling those on the Snake River. Sadly, however, there's no public access to the rim along the deepest parts, and a modest fishing access spot near the Utah Power plant southwest of Grace just doesn't do the canyon justice. But take a peek where you can—some farmers along the Black Canyon Lane southwest of Grace via Turner and Hegstrom Roads might let you look if you ask permission. East of Grace there are interesting interpretive signs detailing how the Last Chance Canal Company struggled to provide irrigation to this region.

Situated off Highway 34 south of the town of Thatcher, **Maple Grove Hot Springs** is a bit farther off the beaten path than other southeastern Idaho thermal retreats, but it's worth the drive. This secluded resort offers daily soaking in several beautiful pools, a variety of campsites, and indoor accommodations in trailers, yurts, and a tiny cabin. The setting is really picturesque, too, on the Oneida Narrows Reservoir of the Bear River, with excellent wildlife watching, fishing, and boating. To get to Maple Grove from Grace, continue south on Highway 34. After 15 miles, watch for 13800 North Rd., and turn left. Make an immediate right on Maple Grove Road and continue south about 3 miles to the hot springs. For more information (including directions from other points in southeastern Idaho), see maplegrovesprings.com or call (208) 851-2126. The address is 11386 North Oneida Narrows Rd., Thatcher.

Most extinct Western towns owed their existence to mining, but **Chesterfield** had its roots in agriculture. Mormon pioneers settled the town in 1880 along the old Oregon Trail. The town reached its peak in the 1920s with a population of about 500 people. After that, however, Chesterfield slowly began to shrink. After World War II, few local boys came home, and the town lost its post office a couple of years later.

No one lives year-round in Chesterfield today, but the town's memory remains remarkably well preserved. About two dozen buildings still stand. The most notable remaining structure is the old Chesterfield LDS Ward meetinghouse, restored as a chapel after serving for years as a museum. The Holbrook Mercantile building serves as a museum and welcome center.

The Chesterfield town site may be toured Mon through Sat, Memorial Day through Labor Day, and RV camping is available, too. Many descendants of early Chesterfield residents come back each Memorial Day for a luncheon and reunion. Nearby Chesterfield Reservoir is a good fishing spot. Chesterfield is located 10 miles north of the town of Bancroft and 15 miles north of US 30. See historicchesterfield.org for information.

Soda Springs, Caribou County's seat and largest town, was a favorite campsite along the Oregon Trail. Many emigrants stopped here to sample water from the area's abundant natural springs. Most are gone now, but evidence remains of two of the most famous. One pioneer spring is preserved under a small pavilion in **Hooper Springs Park,** located 2 miles north of the center of town. "Drink deeply of nature's best beverage," a plaque advises. Hooper Springs is named for W. H. Hooper, who was a leading Salt Lake City banker, Utah congressman, and president of the Zion's Cooperative Mercantile Institution, at one time the Intermountain region's major home-grown department store chain. He had a summer home in Soda Springs and helped the town's soda water reach international markets.

Human-Made Lava

With all the lava in Idaho, you wouldn't think people would pay much heed to another pile of the stuff. Ah, but when it's a human-made lava flow bubbling over the landscape before your eyes—well, that's enough to generate interest. And that's just what happens north of Soda Springs at the Monsanto Chemical Company.

Monsanto, which produces elemental phosphorous—a substance used in laundry detergents, soft drinks, toothpaste, and other products—dumps the resulting slag from its electric furnaces. The slag, 1,400°F hot, fills trucks bearing special cast-steel pots. The trucks then pour the molten rock onto the slag pile five times each hour, twenty-four hours a day. You can almost imagine the local kids asking each other, "Whaddya wanna do tonight, cruise US 30 or go to the slag heap?"

Another spring regularly gave off a sound like that of a steamboat. It's now drowned beneath Alexander Reservoir, but **Steamboat Spring** has not disappeared altogether; on a clear day it can still be viewed puffing and percolating beneath the water's surface. The best way to see evidence of the spring is to play a round on the **Oregon Trail Golf Course.** Look south to the reservoir from either the No. 1 green or the No. 8 tee. From those vantage points you also can see what are probably the only Oregon Trail wagon ruts on a golf course, a phenomenon that was once featured in *National Geographic*. Traces of the wagons' wheels cut across the No. 9 fairway and skirt the No. 1 green before traveling across the No. 8 fairway. Still another famous local spring tasted almost exactly like beer—and produced similar effects once drunk—but it, unfortunately, has vanished completely.

Several other Soda Springs attractions are of particular note. The town has the world's only captive geyser, the centerpiece of the aptly named **Geyser Park.** The gusher was discovered in 1937 as the town attempted to find a hot-water source for its swimming pool. The drill hit the geyser, which was later capped and controlled by a timer. These days it erupts every hour on the hour (unless strong west winds are blowing, which would send the 150-foot-high spray cascading over nearby businesses). The surrounding park offers a pleasant place to rest while waiting for the next "show." You can also view the geyser from the cafe in the **Enders Hotel & Museum** at 76 South Main St. Yes, this is a museum you can sleep in. The budget rooms (about $65 a night) have bathrooms down the hall, while rooms with private baths range from $95 to $195. All have antique period furnishings. Call (208) 547-4980 or see endershotel.org.

Six miles northeast of Soda Springs via Highway 34 and Trail Canyon Road, the Nature Conservancy and the Bureau of Land Management have established a preserve at **Formation Springs.** Here visitors see crystal-clear pools amid a wetlands area at the base of the Aspen Mountains, and wildlife is abundant, too. The springs that feed the pools and nearby creek system deposit high concentrations of calcium carbonate, giving the site its unusual geology. Formation Cave, about 20 feet tall and 1,000 feet long, is among the impressive features. Bring your flashlight!

Bear Lake Country

Two designated scenic routes traverse the state's extreme southeastern corner, intersecting in Soda Springs. The **Pioneer Historic Byway** follows Highway 34 northeast to Wyoming, skirting the shores of Blackfoot Reservoir and Grays Lake, and the south to Preston and Franklin, two of Idaho's oldest towns. The **Oregon Trail–Bear Lake Scenic Byway** runs east from McCammon along US 30 before heading south on US 89 through Montpelier on to Bear Lake, a 20-mile-long recreational paradise straddling the Idaho-Utah border. We'll look at the region following a clockwise direction southeast from Soda Springs and back north toward Pocatello.

Settled in 1864 by Mormon families, Montpelier was named for the capital of Brigham Young's home state, Vermont. Outlaw Butch Cassidy visited here in 1896, joining with two other men in robbing the local bank of $7,165. The bank they supposedly robbed is gone now, but the building in which it stood remains on Washington Street downtown.

Montpelier also is home to the **National Oregon/California Trail Center,** built at the junction of US 30 and 89 at the site known in the 1850s as Clover Creek, a popular emigrant rest stop. Through living history, artwork, and exhibits, the center explains how early travelers made it over the "Big Hill," a nearby ridge that many pioneers considered among the roughest obstacles on the way west; how they lived in the wagon trains; and how they encountered such characters as Thomas "Peg Leg" Smith, a nineteenth-century mountain man who had to amputate his own leg. Smith opened a trading post at what is now Dingle, Idaho, and reportedly made $100 a day catering to the emigrants' needs. The center is open from 9 a.m. to 5 p.m. Mon through Sat and 9 a.m. to 3 p.m. Sun mid-May through Sept. The rest of the year, it's open 10 a.m. to 2 p.m. Mon through Thurs, but there are no living history tours from mid-Oct through mid-May except for groups with advance reservations. Admission is $12 for adults, $11 for seniors 60 and older, $9 for youths ages 8 through 17, and $5 for kids ages 4 to 7. For more information call (866) 847-3800 or see oregontrailcenter.org. The center also is home to the **Rails & Trails Museum,** which showcases other aspects of Bear Lake Valley history.

Although southeast Idaho is geographically and politically part of the Gem State, spiritually the region is closely aligned with Utah and Mormonism. Nowhere is this more true than in the towns and counties bordering the Beehive State. In fact the 1863 settlers who arrived in what was to become Paris, Idaho, thought they were in Utah until an 1872 boundary survey set the record straight.

The imposing and beautiful **Paris Stake Tabernacle** was a labor of love for local Mormon settlers, who spent half a decade building the Romanesque-style church, which was completed in 1889. A *stake* is the term used by the Church of Jesus Christ of Latter-day Saints to describe a geographical area; the Paris, Idaho, stake was the first organized outside the Utah territory, and the tabernacle was built to serve the Mormon communities and congregations that sprung up within a 50-mile radius of the town.

The tabernacle—designed by Joseph Young, a son of Brigham—was built from red sandstone hauled by horse- and ox-drawn wagons from a canyon 18 miles away. In the winter the rock was pulled by sled over frozen Bear Lake. A former shipbuilder crafted the ceiling, using pine harvested in nearby forests. The site is open from 9:30 a.m. to 5:30 p.m. daily Memorial Day through Labor Day. Arrive midday and you may be treated to music from the tabernacle's Austin pipe organ.

A monument on the tabernacle grounds honors Charles Coulson Rich, the man sent by Brigham Young to settle the Bear Lake Valley. It was Rich who, on one of his many missions for the church, went to Europe to find the skilled craftsmen recruited by the Mormons to help build their new churches and towns in the American West. Rich had six wives and fifty children and ultimately became an apostle in his church. Despite Rich's contributions, Paris was named not for him but for Frederick Perris, who platted the town site. One of the first settler cabins, built in 1863 by Thomas Sleight and Charles Atkins, is still standing and may be seen in a park near the tabernacle.

Several intriguing side canyons south of Paris beckon independent-minded motorists from well-traveled US 89. **Bloomington Canyon,** west of the tiny town of the same name, leads to a pristine little lake and meadows filled with wildflowers. **Minnetonka Cave,** located west of St. Charles, is the largest developed limestone cave in Idaho and among the state's more spectacular underground wonderlands. Ninety-minute tours weave through a half-mile of fantastic formations and fossils of preserved tropical plant and marine life in nine separate chambers, the largest of which is about 300 feet around and 90 feet high.

In the late 1930s the federal government began development of Minnetonka Cave via the Works Progress Administration, constructing a trail from

Idaho's "Loch Ness"

Photographers find Bear Lake at its most beautiful at sunrise, when the water frequently glints pink, red, and gold as it catches the waking orb's rays. But locals say sunset visitors are more likely to spy the **Bear Lake Monster,** a serpent-like creature said to live underwater along the lake's east shore. Rumors of the beast have circulated for centuries, first by Native Americans and mountain men, later by Joseph Rich (a son of Mormon pioneer Charles Coulson Rich), who reported his findings in an 1868 article for the *Deseret News* of Salt Lake City. Sightings were especially prevalent around 1900, when people reported strange creatures of up to 90 feet long that could move as fast as running horses.

According to a local tourism brochure, for a long time no one could find a bottom to Bear Lake. People thought perhaps Bear Lake was connected to Scotland by underground tunnels and that the Bear Lake monster was actually the famous Loch Ness monster. Today Bear Lake–area folks speculate the "creature" could be anything from ice formations or a cloud on the water to a large school of fish or elk swimming across the lake. "No one is willing to say if it is real or not," the pamphlet adds. "That is up to you to decide. But be on the lookout for the monster, and please report any sightings."

St. Charles Canyon and installing interior paths, steps, and railings. But the cave was open only for a couple of years before World War II began, halting efforts at improvement. After the war the Paris Lions Club operated the cave for a time. It is now managed by the US Forest Service as part of the Caribou-Targhee National Forest. Tours of Minnetonka Cave are given every half-hour from 10 a.m. to 5:30 p.m. each day from around Memorial Day through Labor Day. The cost is $8 for adults, $6 for children ages 6 through 15, or $32 for a family. Children ages 5 and under get in free. Visitors should be prepared for lots of steps and cool temperatures. Good walking shoes and a jacket are recommended, but be sure to wear and carry things that haven't been taken into other caves. (The Forest Service is trying to limit the spread of a bat disease known as white-nose syndrome.) Several campgrounds are available up St. Charles Canyon. For more information on the cave or surrounding forest, call (435) 245-4422 or see fs.usda.gov/ctnf.

St. Charles serves as gateway to **Bear Lake,** one of the bluest bodies of water in North America. Explanations for its turquoise tint vary, but it's usually credited to a high concentration of soluble carbonates. Bear Lake also is unique because it boasts several species of fish found nowhere else. In addition to the rainbow and cutthroat trout so plentiful throughout the Rockies, Bear Lake is home to the Bonneville cisco, a sardine-like whitefish that spawns each January and is popular year-round for bait. (You can catch and keep up to thirty of them a day in season.) Learn more about park activities and services at parksandrecreation.idaho.gov/parks/bear-lake.

In addition to fish, Bear Lake country is thick with animals and birds. The **Bear Lake National Wildlife Refuge** at the lake's north end draws Canada geese; sandhill and whooping cranes; redhead, canvasback, and mallard ducks; and the nation's largest nesting population of white-face ibis. Deer, moose, and smaller mammals are also known to wander through the refuge's 19,000 acres. Check with the refuge office in Montpelier or call (208) 847-1757 for information on waterfowl hunting, boating, and hiking opportunities.

The Utah end of Bear Lake is far more commercially developed than Idaho's shores. Bear Lake Boulevard in and near Garden City, Utah, is lined with resorts and restaurants, but there are very few visitor services north of the border. That's one reason **The Bluebird Inn** stands out. The inn is a good base for summer lake activities, but it's also popular with winter sports enthusiasts, with a 380-mile network of snowmobile trails located nearby. Five rooms (each with a private bath and fireplace) rent for $150 to $175. For more information call (800) 797-6448 or see thebluebirdinn.com.

Southwest of Bear Lake, US 89 makes a scenic 45-mile swing through the Wasatch National Forest and Logan Canyon before meeting US 91 at Logan. From there it's a short drive back north into Idaho, where our explorations continue at Franklin. (For more information on the Beehive State, check out *Utah Off the Beaten Path.*)

Franklin, founded in 1860, beats out Paris for the title of Idaho's oldest settled town by three years. But like the pioneers at Paris, Franklin's early townsfolk thought they were part of Utah until the 1872 survey confirmed the town's location in what was to become the state of Idaho. Franklin's museum is called the **Relic Hall,** and it houses many artifacts and photos of pioneer life. A park complete with picnic grounds and a fireplace now surrounds the hall. Two of Franklin's most interesting sights are located just outside of town on the Old Yellowstone Highway. (Turn west at the Daughters of the Utah Pioneers marker north of town.) The ruins on the north side of the road are those of what is likely the **oldest flour mill** in the state of Idaho. And just across the road, the **Yellowstone Rock** shows the old route to the nation's first national park. After Yellowstone received its national park designation, large boulders with arrows pointing the way were placed along what was then the main road to the park to help travelers find their way. This may be the last such marker still in existence.

The scenic **Cub River Canyon** east of US 91 between Franklin and Preston is home to the **Cub River Guest Ranch.** Family-run since 1940, this year-round retreat offers rooms in a guest lodge, rustic cabins, and camping.

Amenities include a swimming pool, hot tub, theater room, catered meals for groups, and more. Call (208) 852-2124 or see cubriverguestranch.com for details on accommodations. A neighboring restaurant, the **Deer Cliff Inn,** features streamside patio dining and dancing in the summer and some late spring and autumn weekends. Drive on up the canyon for beautiful Wasatch Mountain scenery, especially in fall when the maples turn a dazzling red.

Brigham Young, the Mormon leader, urged his followers to heed the golden rule when dealing with Native Americans. "Treat them in all respects as you would like to be treated," he said in an 1852 speech. Indeed the Mormons who settled Idaho early on made pacts with the local chiefs to share crops and live together peacefully. Still there were tensions, and they boiled over in January 1863 in the **Battle of Bear River** 2.5 miles north of Preston. More Native Americans died in this little-known incident than in any other; there were more casualties—as many as 400 men, women, and children killed—than at Wounded Knee, Sand Creek, or Little Big Horn. The battle was triggered by the death of a miner on Bear River during a Native attack; Colonel Patrick Connor of the Third California Infantry, stationed at Fort Douglas near Salt Lake City, used the incident as an excuse to make war. William Hull, a local pioneer who witnessed the battle, gave this account of its aftermath: "Never will I forget the scene, dead bodies were everywhere. I counted eight deep in one place and in several places they were three to five deep. In all we counted nearly 400; two-thirds of this number being women and children." A monument along the east side of US 91 north of Preston makes note of the battle, and the actual battle site was nearby along aptly named Battle Creek.

Not far north of the Battle of Bear River site, another wayside commemorates **Red Rock Pass.** It was through here that prehistoric Bonneville Lake breached its shores about 14,500 years ago, unleashing one of history's greatest floods.

Gosh! Preston is Flippin' Sweet!

If you've seen the indie film hit **Napoleon Dynamite,** you're probably wondering whether Preston is anything like the slightly time-warped town seen in the movie. The answer is: Heck, yes! If you come to Preston, you really will see such landmarks as the King's store where Summer Wheatley works, the Pop'N Pins bowling alley where Kip and Uncle Rico plot their business empire, and the Deseret Industries Thrift Store where Napoleon buys the awesome leisure suit he wears to the big dance. You can even stay overnight at the Plaza Motel, where the cast and crew bunked while making the movie.

A pilgrimage to Preston is a must for *Dynamite* devotees, but even casual fans will enjoy a visit. Search for *Napoleon Dynamite* at movie-locations.com to see photos and addresses of sites including Pedro's house and Preston High School.

Malad City, the Oneida County seat, had one of the nation's first JCPenney stores at 59 North Main St. *Malad* is French for "sick," and—like the Malad Gorge and Malad River in South Central Idaho—Malad City and its nearby (and much longer) Malad River reportedly earned their names when a party of trappers became sick after drinking from the stream. But those early trappers probably didn't feel nearly as sick as did Glispie Waldron, who, in 1890, may have blown his chance at finding a buried treasure.

It seems that during the 1860s and 1870s, Malad City was a major stop for freight wagons taking supplies from Utah north to the mines of Idaho and Montana, as well as those returning with gold. This traffic also made Malad a favorite target of robbers and other ne'er-do-wells, one group of which reportedly hid the loot from a stagecoach holdup somewhere in the Samaria Mountains located southwest of town, planning to retrieve it later. Waldron was traveling in the area in 1890 when he reportedly spied an iron door covering a cave. He tied his coat to a nearby tree to mark the spot, intending to return. But he didn't make it back for a couple of years, and by then, his coat was gone. To this day treasure seekers are still searching for the fabled iron door and the riches that may lie behind it. If you're interested in trying your own luck, stop by the **Oneida County Pioneer Museum** at 27 Bannock St. in Malad City for tips on where to look. It's open 1 to 5 p.m. Tues through Sat during the summer months.

If you haven't had your fill of Southeastern Idaho water recreation by now, check out **Downata Hot Springs Resort,** located near the town of Downey. Aside from pools, waterslides, and a water playground, this year-round resort offers a restaurant (with weekend "steak and soak" specials), RV and tent camping, indoor lodging, and a spa. Downey is on US 91, 6 miles south of its junction with I-15. Call (208) 897-5736 for hours and more information or see downatahotsprings.com.

Places to Stay in Southeastern Idaho

AMERICAN FALLS

Fairview Inn Bed & Breakfast
2998 Fairview Lane
(208) 226-2060
fairviewinnbedand
breakfast.com
Moderate

BLACKFOOT

Best Western Blackfoot Inn
750 Jensen Grove Dr.
(208) 785-4144
bestwesternidaho.com
Moderate

Super 8 Blackfoot
1279 Parkway Dr.
(208) 785-9333
super8.com
Moderate

POCATELLO

AmeriTel Inn
1440 Bench Rd.
(208) 234-7500
ameritelinns.com
Moderate–Expensive

Black Swan Inn
746 East Center
(208) 233-3051
blackswaninn.com
Moderate–Expensive

Comfort Inn
1333 Bench Rd.
(208) 237-8155
choicehotels.com
Moderate

HELPFUL WEBSITES FOR SOUTHEASTERN IDAHO

Bear River Heritage Area
bearriverheritage.com

City of Pocatello
pocatello.us

Greater Pocatello Chamber of Commerce
pocatelloidaho.com

Idaho State Journal **(Pocatello newspaper)**
idahostatejournal.com

Lava Hot Springs tourism
lavahotsprings.org

Shoshone-Bannock Tribes
shoshonebannocktribes.com

Holiday Inn Express & Suites
200 Via Venitio
(208) 478-9800
hiexpress.com
Expensive

Motel 6
291 West Burnside Ave.
(Chubbuck)
motel6.com
Inexpensive

Red Lion Hotel
1555 Pocatello Creek Rd.
(208) 233-2200
redlion.com/pocatello
Moderate

MCCAMMON

Harkness Hotel
206 Center St.
(208) 254-4340
theharknesshotel.com
Moderate–Expensive

LAVA HOT SPRINGS

Home Hotel
306 East Main St.
(208) 776-5050
homehotel.com
Moderate–Expensive

Lava Hot Springs Inn
94 East Portneuf
(208) 776-5830
lavahotspringsinn.com
Moderate–Expensive

Riverside Inn & Hot Springs
255 East Portneuf
(208) 776 5504
riversideinnhotsprings.com
Moderate–Expensive

SODA SPRINGS

Enders Hotel & Museum
76 South Main St.
(208) 547-4980
endershotel.org
Inexpensive–Moderate

Trail Canyon Lodge
3367 Trail Canyon Rd.
(208) 547-3828
trailcanyonlodge.com
Inexpensive–Moderate

MONTPELIER

Clover Creek Inn
243 North Fourth St.
(208) 847-1782
clovercreekinn.com
Moderate

Rest Assured Inns & Suites
745 Washington St.
(208) 847-1911
restassuredinns.com
Moderate

FISH HAVEN

The Bluebird Inn
423 US 89
(208) 945-2571
thebluebirdinn.com
Expensive

PRESTON

Plaza Motel
427 South US 91
(208) 852 2020
Inexpensive

Places to Eat in Southeastern Idaho

AMERICAN FALLS

China City
220 Harrison
(208) 226-7038
Inexpensive

ALSO WORTH SEEING IN SOUTHEASTERN IDAHO

American Falls Reservoir
north of American Falls

Bingham County Historical Museum
Blackfoot

Idaho Museum of Natural History
Pocatello

Pebble Creek Ski Area
Pocatello

Grays Lake National Wildlife Refuge
north of Soda Springs

Tres Hermanos
(Mexican)
2854 Pocatello Ave.
(208) 226-2223
Inexpensive

BLACKFOOT

El Mirador
(Mexican)
620 West Bridge St.
(208) 785-1595
Inexpensive

Homestead Family Restaurant
(American)
1355 Parkway Dr.
(208) 785-0700
Inexpensive–Moderate

Martha's Cafe
(American)
851 South Broadway
(208) 785-4199
Inexpensive

POCATELLO

The Bridge
(New American)
815 South First Ave.
(208) 234-7000
Moderate

Buddy's Italian Restaurant
626 East Lewis
(208) 233-1172
Inexpensive–Moderate

Efresh
(salads/sandwiches)
302 East Center
(208) 242-3747
Inexpensive

Goody's Deli
(pizza/sandwiches)
905 South Fifth Ave.
(208) 233-9210
Inexpensive–Moderate

Grecian Key
(Greek)
314 North Main St.
(208) 235-3922
Inexpensive

Mama Inez
(Mexican)
390 Yellowstone Ave.
(208) 234-7674
Inexpensive–Moderate

Mocha Madness
(coffeehouse)
546 South Fifth Ave.
(208) 233-2380
Inexpensive

Portneuf Valley Brewing Company
(American)
615 North First Ave.
(208) 232-1644
Moderate

LAVA HOT SPRINGS

Portneuf Grille & Lounge
(fine dining)
255 East Portneuf St.
(208) 776-5504
Moderate–Expensive

Riverwalk Cafe
(Thai)
695 East Main St.
(208) 776-5872
Inexpensive

SODA SPRINGS

Arctic Circle
(fast food)
100 East Second South
(208) 547-3635
Inexpensive

Geyser View Restaurant
(American)
76 South Main St.
(208) 547-4980
Moderate

MONTPELIER

Ranch Hand Trail Stop
(truck stop diner)
23200 US 30
(208) 847-1180
Inexpensive–Moderate

PRESTON

Big J Burgers
(fast food)
196 North State St.
(208) 852-2800
Inexpensive

Deer Cliff Inn
(American)
up Cub River Canyon
(208) 852-0643
Inexpensive–Moderate

MALAD CITY

Me 'n' Lou's Diner
(American)
75 South 300 East
(208) 766-2919
Inexpensive–Moderate

Eastern Idaho

In Eastern Idaho the outdoors are never far away. This is the western gateway to two of America's premier national parks, as well as to swift-running rivers and backcountry byways. Mountain peaks and massive buttes rim every horizon, shadowing the fertile, irrigated fields.

The region is defined by three routes: I-15, busy around Idaho Falls, then rather lonely on its trek north to Montana; US 20, which carries traffic to West Yellowstone, one of Yellowstone National Park's major entrances; and US 26, a popular route to Jackson Hole and Grand Teton National Park. As might be expected, summertime traffic is thick on US 20 and 26. Fortunately, several possible alternatives give travelers the chance to break away from the pack or make a loop tour of the region. The most popular of these, the Teton Scenic Byway and adjacent Mesa Falls Scenic Byway, are still well traveled—yet on these routes, you'll complete your trip feeling you've at least seen something other than the bumper of the vehicle in front of you.

For additional Eastern Idaho travel information, call (800) 634-3246 or (208) 356-5700 or see yellowstoneteton.org.

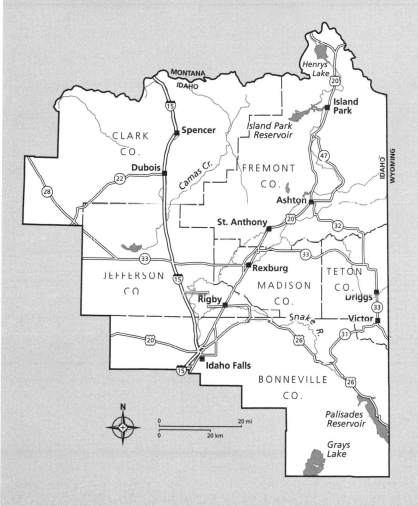

The Upper Snake River

Even within the city limits of Idaho Falls, nature makes her presence known. Unlike Twin Falls, where a set of Snake River cascades gave the town its name, Idaho Falls got its name before any falls really existed. The city of about 57,000 people started life as Eagle Rock, taking that name from a ferry built in 1863 by Bill Hickman and Harry Rickards. (The ferry was positioned near a small rock island on which bald eagles frequently nested in a juniper tree.) In its early days Eagle Rock served as a major fording point for miners heading to the riches of central and western Idaho; the community also was known as Taylor's Crossing or Taylor's Bridge for the early span built by James "Matt" Taylor. Later, Eagle Rock served as the center of railroad activity in the new Idaho Territory, but all that changed in 1887 when the Union Pacific moved its headquarters south to Pocatello and Eagle Rock's population plummeted. By 1891 a team of Chicago developers—Charles N. Lee, W. G. Emerson, D. W. Higbee, J. B. Holmes, and Bernard McCaffery—had descended on Eagle Rock. Seeing the rapids on the Snake River, they encouraged the locals to change the town's name to Idaho Falls. But it was not until 1911 that human-made falls were completed, giving the city legitimate claim to its name.

Since then Idaho Falls has made good use of its riverside location. The *Idaho Falls Greenbelt* runs several miles north and south of downtown. It's a pleasant place for downtown workers to spend their lunch hour, and on weekends local residents flock to its paths and parks to enjoy a run, bike ride, or picnic. Another good outdoor destination, especially with children, is the *Idaho Falls Zoo* at Tautphaus Park. Exhibits include an Australian outback area, a bi-level otter home, penguins, zebras, a children's petting zoo, a pond filled with Idaho waterfowl, and an "Asian Adventure" exhibit with sloth bears, red-crowned cranes, and snow leopards. Zoo admission is $7.50 for age 13 and up, $4.50 for children ages 4 through 12, and $6 for seniors age

AUTHOR'S FAVORITES IN EASTERN IDAHO

Museum of Idaho Idaho Falls	**Idaho Centennial Carousel** Rexburg
Idaho Falls Zoo Idaho Falls	**Mesa Falls Scenic Byway** near Ashton
Farnsworth TV & Pioneer Museum Rigby	**Harriman State Park** near Island Park

62 and up. Children age 3 and under get in free. Summer hours (Memorial Day through Labor Day) are 9 a.m. to 5 p.m. daily (with evening hours on the first Fri of July, Aug, and Sept). Mid-Apr through Memorial Day weekend and Labor Day weekend through early Oct, the zoo is open daily from 9 a.m. to 4 p.m. The closing times noted here are when the last admission is sold; the zoo gates remain open an hour after that. The zoo is closed the rest of the year. Tautphaus Park is between Rollandet Avenue and South Boulevard east of Yellowstone Avenue in south Idaho Falls. Call (208) 612-8552 or see idahofallszoo.org for updates.

There's plenty to see in downtown Idaho Falls, starting with the **Museum of Idaho,** which incorporated and expanded upon the former Bonneville County Historical Museum in the old Carnegie Library. Featured shows here have included explorations of everything from guitars to space travel to dinosaurs, while permanent exhibits include a walk-through replica of the town of Eagle Rock as it may have appeared in 1891; a children's discovery area; and displays showing Eastern Idaho's role as a major region for nuclear energy research. (The Idaho National Laboratory west of Idaho Falls is among the state's largest employers.) The museum, located at 200 North Eastern Ave., is generally open from 9 a.m. to 8 p.m. Mon and Tues and 9 a.m. to 5 p.m. Wed through Sat, though hours vary as new exhibits are staged, so check before a visit. Admission is $9 for adults, $8 for seniors age 62 and up, and $7 for youths age 18 and under. Family passes cost $30 ($25 on Mon night). For more information call (208) 522-1400 or see museumofidaho.org.

The city's landmark structure is the **Idaho Falls Temple** of the Church of Jesus Christ of Latter-day Saints, located along the Snake River at 1000 Memorial Dr., its spire visible for miles. The temple's visitor center is open daily from 9 a.m. to 9 p.m. Free tours are available, and exhibits highlight Mormon history, art, and culture.

For more architectural highlights, the Idaho Falls Historic Preservation Committee has prepared several informative pamphlets detailing walking tours. For example, the **Ridge Avenue Historic District** has sixty-seven notable buildings, with styles ranging from Queen Anne to Craftsman to Colonial Revival. One of the most auspicious structures on the tour is the **First Presbyterian Church** at 325 Elm St., a neoclassical building complete with Roman dome and Ionic portico. Pick up brochures at area visitor centers and museums.

Idaho Falls has a vibrant arts scene. **The Art Museum of Eastern Idaho** has a lovely riverside home at 300 South Capital Ave., where it presents changing exhibits and many special events. Hours are 11 a.m. to 5 p.m. Tues through Sat, with extended hours on Thurs evening until 8 p.m. (There are gallery walks throughout downtown the first Thurs evening of each month.) Admission is $4 for adults, $2 for youths ages 6 to 17 and college students with ID, and $10 for a family. Everyone gets in for free the first Sat of the month.

The Idaho Falls Arts Council has its headquarters in the ***Colonial Theater and Willard Arts Center*** at 450 A St. Broadway shows and touring musicians come here frequently. The center has a regular menu of arts classes for children and adults, and two galleries showcase the work of artists from around the state. The arts council also runs the ***ARTitorium on Broadway,*** an interactive arts and technology playground for all ages at 271 West Broadway. It's open from 10 a.m. to 6 p.m. Tues through Sat with additional hours during school breaks. Admission is $5 a person, free for kids under age 3. Call (208) 552-1080 or see artitoriumonbroadway.org for more information. For a look at the arts council's upcoming events, see idahofallsarts.org.

Across the street from the arts center at 439 A St., ***BlackRock*** is an upscale casual bar featuring thirty beer taps, a selection of wine, and frequent live music. If a full meal is what you have in mind, there are plenty of good choices nearby. ***Diablas Kitchen*** at 368 A St. specializes in fresh food for lunch, theme dinners, and takeaway healthy comfort food supper selections Tues through Thurs. ***The Snake Bite*** at 401 Park Ave. is a longtime favorite. Try the Blue Snake burger with bleu cheese and mild green chili peppers, or the house salad with bleu cheese and cranberry salsa. ***Grandpa's Southern Barbecue*** at 545 Shoup Ave. has devoted fans from all over southern Idaho who say it serves the best barbecue in the state. Save room for a slice of sweet potato pie.

Among the many interesting shops in the downtown core, ***WeeBee Toys*** at 492 Shoup Ave. is a standout, with its K'nex creations and colorful ceiling

Neat Seats

If you get tired walking around Idaho Falls, a bench will probably be close at hand—and not just any bench, either. In 2005 the city arts council, the Idaho Falls Historic Downtown Foundation, and the City of Idaho Falls teamed up to install **Art You Can Sit On,** twenty regionally inspired public benches around the city center.

More than a dozen different artists created the benches from concrete, wood, bronze, copper, marble, and river rock. Designs range from the whimsical (see the "Skateboard" bench by Carol Popenga at Park and A Streets) to the sublime ("Rest Surprise" by Lisa Bade at the Idaho Falls Public Library at 457 West Broadway St.). Eastern Idaho's natural beauty and wildlife are well represented, too, in such benches as "Trout" by Davidjohn Stosich at Shoup Avenue and A Street and "Geese" by Marilyn H. Hansen on the 400 block of A Street. Stop by the arts council office for a walking tour brochure featuring the "sculptural seats."

TOP ANNUAL EVENTS IN EASTERN IDAHO

Idaho Falls Chukars baseball
(June–Sept)

Fourth of July Events
Idaho Falls

Summer Festival
Teton Valley (early July)

Idaho International Summerfest
Rexburg (late July–early Aug)

Grand Targhee Bluegrass Music
Grand Targhee (mid-Aug)

banners, and ***Chesboro Music*** at 327 West Broadway has been going strong since 1911. Chesboro mainly aims to keep Eastern Idaho kids in band instruments and sheet music, but it has plenty of musical toys and classes for everyone.

Idaho Falls has many national chain hotels, including several with commanding locations on the Greenbelt, and they fill up fast in summer with people traveling to and from the national parks. For something a bit different, ***Destinations Inn*** at 295 West Broadway has fourteen themed suites in a renovated century-old building. Guests can pretend they're spending the night in Rome, Rio, Thailand, or another exotic locale. Rates start at $119 on weekdays and $159 on weekends, with a weekly special posted every Monday on the inn's Facebook page. Get more info at destinationsinn.com or call (208) 528-8444. A sister property in Pocatello, the Black Swan Inn, has similar themed suites.

US 26, the road from Idaho Falls to Grand Teton National Park, isn't exactly off the beaten path. Sometimes in our hurry to get somewhere else, however, we miss seeing something interesting right along our way. Such is the case with the big, unusual looking building at 4523 US 26, a few miles north of Idaho Falls. For years I drove by wondering. Was it a school? A barn? Actually, it was both: a school built in 1899 and a barn erected shortly thereafter. Both structures now sit on the same site and serve as home to the ***Country Store Boutique,*** a shop boasting 15,000 square feet of the old, new, and unusual. Unlike many shops featuring antiques and collectibles, the Country Store Boutique doesn't feel musty and overstuffed. There's room to move around amid the solid old wood furniture, the antique glassware, and the Native American pottery and jewelry. The boutique also carries quilts, rugs, baskets, arrowheads, sheet music, folk art, and more. It's a great place to shop for a gift or for your home. The store is open 10 a.m. to 6 p.m. Mon through Sat. Call (208) 522-8450 for more information, and see recent finds on the store's Facebook page.

Do you watch television? If so, you may want to make a pilgrimage to Rigby, hometown of ***Philo T. Farnsworth,*** who invented the cathode-ray tube and made TV possible. No couch potato, Farnsworth was a natural whiz at all things mechanical. Born in Utah in 1906, he moved to a farm near Rigby when he was a boy. Fascinated by electricity, he played violin in a dance orchestra to earn money for books on the topic. Farnsworth was 14 years old when he got the idea for TV while plowing a field, and one day he sketched out his ideas on a blackboard at Rigby High School. By 1927 Farnsworth—then living in California—was able to prove his idea worked by transmitting a single horizontal line from a camera in one room to a receiving screen in another. He was just 21.

In 1930 electronics giant RCA offered to buy Farnsworth's invention for a cool $200,000 and give him a job, but the inventor—preferring to preserve his independence—turned them down flat. That refusal apparently triggered the patent war between Farnsworth and RCA, which claimed one of its own employees, Vladimir Zworykin, had actually invented television. Zworykin had been tinkering with TV, but it wasn't until he visited Farnsworth's lab and saw the Idaho native's invention that he was able to duplicate Philo's principles and work. RCA eventually filed suit against Farnsworth, but the inventor prevailed, especially after his former high-school science teacher produced a 1922 sketch of Philo's television theory.

Farnsworth never finished high school, yet by the time he died in 1971 he had earned 300 patents and an honorary doctorate from Brigham Young University. His other notable inventions included the baby incubator, and at the time of his death, he was working on the theory of nuclear fission. Zworykin still sometimes gets credit for Farnsworth's television invention, but the truth is coming out—and someday Farnsworth's name may be as famous as those of fellow inventors Thomas Edison and Alexander Graham Bell.

The ***Jefferson County Museum,*** better known as the ***Farnsworth TV & Pioneer Museum,*** has extensive displays about the inventor's life and work, including several handwritten journals, his Dictaphone (another Farnsworth television), much of his science book collection, and copies of just about anything ever written about the inventor. Other exhibits detail the early history of Jefferson County and its communities, including a Hall of Fame honoring local boys author Vardis Fisher and NFL great Larry Wilson. You also can see a jar of peaches canned in 1886! Museum hours are from 1 to 5 p.m. Tues through Sat or by appointment. Suggested donation is $2 for adults and $1 for children. The museum is at 118 West First South in Rigby; just look for the high tower. The phone number is (208) 745-8423.

East of Idaho Falls near Ririe, ***Heise Hot Springs*** features a swimming pool with waterslide and a soothing 105°F mineral hot bath. Visitors also can camp amid tall cottonwood trees, tee off on a nine-hole par twenty-nine golf course, grab a bite at the pizza parlor, or spread a picnic on the lawn. For more adventurous souls, Heise Zip includes ten zip lines over more than a mile of terrain. Heise Hot Springs is open year-round except for about three weeks for pool maintenance in Nov. For more information or current hours, call (208) 538-7312 or see heisehotsprings.net.

Mountain River Ranch, also near Ririe, offers down-home dinner theater entertainment in high summer (late June through Labor Day weekend) and from Thanksgiving weekend through December. Ride to the vittles on a hay wagon or sleigh, then enjoy dinner and the show. Depending on the season and your choice of meal, the experience costs about $30 to $50 for adults and $20 to $30 for kids ages 4 through 12. In summer the ranch has a fee-fishing pond (no license needed), an RV park, and cabins and rooms for rent. For more information call (208) 538-7337 or see mountainriverranch.com.

The *Cress Creek Nature Trail* is another worthy stop east of Ririe off the Heise Road. This well-marked path gives visitors a chance to learn about the flora, fauna, and geology of Eastern Idaho, all while enjoying some tremendous views. At one point the panorama stretches from the Caribou Mountain Range south of the Snake River all the way to the Beaverhead Range on the Montana border. The Blackfoot Mountains, Big Southern Butte and East Twin Butte, the Lost River Mountain Range, and the Menan Buttes can all be seen as well.

US 26 continues to follow the Upper Snake River toward its origin in Wyoming. The Swan Valley–Palisades area is one of Eastern Idaho's least populated and most scenic stretches. Several US Forest Service campgrounds along Palisades Reservoir provide excellent bases for enjoying the region's good fishing and boating.

The *Lodge at Palisades Creek* is considered one of the top fly-fishing lodges in the West. This rustic-yet-elegant, Orvis-endorsed resort sits within casting distance of the South Fork of the Snake River and Palisades Creek, and the fly-fishing is so good that dinner is served until 10 p.m. to accommodate guests who wish to stay in the river well into the evening. Accommodations options include nine log cabins and a two-bedroom chalet, all overlooking the river. The lodge is spendy, as we say here in Idaho—$215 to $550 per person per day, double occupancy, including breakfast and dinner, beverages, and lodge activities, but not including guide service. Non-guests can come for dinner by reservation. For more information call (208) 483-2222 or see tlapc.com.

At Swan Valley, the traveler has a choice: Continue on US 26 to Alpine, Wyoming (the southern gateway to Jackson Hole), or take Highway 31 over Pine Creek Pass, elevation 6,764 feet. The latter provides access to Idaho's Teton Valley, the area we will explore next.

I Scream, You Scream . . .

The heavily Mormon country of Eastern Idaho and Utah reportedly has some of the highest ice-cream consumption rates in the United States. Some theorize this is because members of the Church of Jesus Christ of Latter-day Saints deny themselves other hedonistic pleasures like alcohol and caffeine. But it may also simply be because there's a lot of excellent ice cream made by places like **Reed's Dairy,** located on the western outskirts of Idaho Falls at 2660 West Broadway (just west of Broadway and Bellin, on the north side). Reed's makes about fifty flavors, including such favorites as Moo Tracks (vanilla with peanut butter and chocolate chips) and Chunky Monkey (banana with nuts and chocolate chips). You'll usually have your pick of eighteen at any one time. Cones, shakes, sundaes, frozen yogurt, and grilled cheese sandwiches are available; there is informal seating inside and out; and self-guided tours are offered, too. Reed's Dairy is open Mon through Sat from 8 a.m. to 9 p.m. There's a second shop at 2523 East Sunnyside Rd. in Ammon (a few miles east of Idaho Falls). See more at reedsdairy.com.

The **Rainey Creek Country Store** is another can't-miss spot on the region's ice-cream circuit. This convenience store at the junction of US 26 and Highway 31 is famous for serving square ice-cream cones. Actually, it's the ice cream that is square—not the cones—but you get the idea. Rainey Creek offers twenty-four flavors, including huckleberries-and-cream, the favorite, and it's open from about 7 a.m. to 8 p.m. (9 p.m. in summer) so you can get a cool fix pretty much anytime you're driving by. In fact, there are only two legitimate excuses for passing up Rainey Creek: You are a diabetic or otherwise unable to eat ice cream, or you plan to head over Pine Creek Pass for a huckleberry shake in Victor.

Teton Valley

Wyoming's Teton Range ranks among the world's most magnificent chains of mountains. The classic view of the Tetons is from the east, but Idaho's Teton Valley offers a less-crowded, equally scenic approach to the famed peaks. Highways 31, 33, and 32 (in that order, from south to north) have been designated Idaho's **Teton Scenic Byway.** Along the way the drive winds through several small towns—Victor, Driggs, and Tetonia—oriented to outdoor recreation.

The **Teton Geotourism Center** at 60 South Main St. in Victor was developed with the inspiration of *National Geographic*. It's worth a stop for maps, travel-planning ideas, and interactive exhibits showing how the Teton Valley's spectacular geography continues to shape the region's heritage and culture.

The **Victor Emporium** at 45 North Main St. is an old-fashioned soda fountain known for its huckleberry milkshakes. It also sells sandwiches, along with fishing gear and Idaho souvenirs. For adult beverages and craft sodas,

Grand Teton Brewing has been in business since 1988, and its pub is open daily just south of Victor at 430 Old Jackson Hwy. Victor is the setting for a fun summer music series, *Music on Main,* held every Thurs from late June through mid-Aug at its city park. Touring bands pair with local favorites, and the music starts at 6 p.m.

Driggs is the jumping-off spot for *Grand Targhee Resort,* just over the border in Alta, Wyoming, but accessible only via the Tetons' Idaho side. Targhee is well known for getting a pile of snow, typically more than 500 inches each winter, including plenty of powder on its 2,600 acres. There are plenty of programs for skiers and snowboarders of all levels. Targhee is definitely a target of extreme skiers, and it was one of the first resorts to add fat-tire biking in winter.

Grand Targhee is worth a visit in warmer weather, too. Take the chairlift to the top of Fred's Mountain for a great Teton vista. There's also a mountain bike park, horseback riding, disc golf, tennis, hiking, swimming, a climbing wall, and a bungee trampoline, plus activities and child care for kids of all ages. Resort staff can arrange a fly-fishing, river-rafting, or soaring expedition nearby. Grand Targhee is also the site for several summer music festivals including Targhee Fest in July and the long-running Grand Targhee Bluegrass Festival in mid-Aug, preceded by a music camp. For more information on Grand Targhee, call (800) TARGHEE or see grandtarghee.com.

The Teton Valley has several unusual spots to bed down for one night or longer. *The Pines Motel–Guest Haus* at 105 South Main in Driggs, is a European-inspired combination of mom-and-pop motel and bed-and-breakfast inn. Originally a two-story log cabin built about 1900, the building has been enlarged to include nine rooms priced from $65 to $85 a night. (A two-room suite costs $120.) Pets are permitted for an additional $10 nightly. A few of the less-expensive rooms share a bathroom. Many travelers who stay at the Pines seem to wind up part of John and Nancy Nielson's extended clan, returning for holiday dinners and corresponding with the family. Outdoors, a stone fireplace, gas grill, lawn chairs, and play area offer summertime fun and relaxation. For more information or reservations, call (800) 354-2778 or see thepinestetonvalley.com.

Set at the base of the road to Teton Pass, *Moose Creek Ranch* is another good option for families exploring the Tetons region. Set on eighteen acres, Moose Creek has accommodations ranging from luxury tents to a ranch house, with rates from $110 to $425 a night. Horseback rides are available, priced from $45 for an hour in the saddle to $150 for a full day on the trail. For more information call (208) 787-6078 or see moosecreekranch.com.

Drive-In Delights

If you grew up in the '50s, '60s, or '70s, chances are you spent your share of summer nights parked in front of a massive outdoor movie screen, either fighting with your siblings or smooching with your sweetie. Drive-in movie theaters are dying out across much of North America, but the Gem State still has quite a few.

Appropriately enough for Idaho, the one just south of Driggs at 2175 South Highway 33 is called the **Spud Drive-In.** The Spud's giant potato is a landmark throughout the region, and its hamburgers are pretty famous, too. For twenty-four-hour movie information, call (208) 354-2727 or see spuddrivein.com. Elsewhere in Idaho, you'll still find drive-in theaters at Caldwell, Grangeville, Idaho Falls, Parma, Pocatello, and Rexburg.

Yellowstone Country

Just west of Tetonia the Teton Scenic Byway continues north on Highway 32, terminating in Ashton, where the Mesa Falls Scenic Byway begins. This stretch of the byway roughly parallels the Ashton-Tetonia Trail, a 30-mile recreational gravel path that follows the abandoned railroad bed of the Teton Valley Branch of the Union Pacific Railroad. Highlights include several restored railroad bridges and trestles, plus views of the Teton Range if you ride from Ashton to Tetonia. Get more info at parksandrecreation.idaho.gov/parks/ashton-tetonia-trail.

Highway 33 continues west to Rexburg, the largest city in the Teton Valley. En route plan a stop at the **Teton Dam Site,** just a mile and a half north of Highway 33 near Newdale. A big pyramid of earth is all that is left of the Teton Dam, which collapsed June 5, 1976, killing eleven people and causing nearly $1 billion in damage. (The nearby Idaho state highway historical marker erroneously puts the death toll at fourteen.) The dam—widely opposed by environmentalists—had just been completed and its reservoir was still being filled when the breach occurred, unleashing 80 billion gallons of water toward Wilford, Sugar City, Rexburg, and Idaho Falls. Fortunately most Teton Valley residents heard about the coming torrent and were able to evacuate before the waters swept through their towns.

The **Teton Flood Museum,** at 51 North Center St. in Rexburg, tells the tale in exhibits, photos, and a fascinating video called *One Saturday Morning*. (Ask at the front desk to view it.) Other displays at the museum showcase handmade quilts and a collection of more than 300 salt-and-pepper shakers. A children's museum is here, too. The Teton Flood Museum is open from 10 a.m. to 5 p.m. Mon through Sat from May through Sept (with extended hours until 7 p.m. Mon) and 11 a.m. to 7 p.m. Mon and 11 a.m. to 5 p.m. Tues